Hello

The iPad is the most remarkable product in Apple's whole line-up. It's got us pretty excited, as you can probably tell...

The original iPad was an extraordinary success. More imitators than anyone could have imagined have spent the last year chasing its tail, but none has come close to matching its stunning performance. During its first nine months on the shelves Apple sold an incredible 15 million units of the original iPad, while the number of applications written to specifically take advantage of its larger screen had grown to 65,000 by early 2011.

A follow-up was all but guaranteed.

Now that follow-up has arrived. Steve Jobs unveiled iPad 2 on 2nd March to an invited audience of technology and lifestyle journalists, in a packed Californian theatre. Such is the global interest in the product, and so great the impact of the original edition, that the event was simulcast to carbon-copy gatherings around the world.

iPad 2 exceeded many viewers' hopes.

With a brand new Apple A5 processor, it is twice as fast as its predecessor and has massively improved graphics performance. Apple claims that in this area alone it is nine times faster than the original iPad.

As before there are six models in the range, each with wifi and, for three of them, 3G connections to the outside world. They all run the latest version of Apple's mobile operating system – iOS 4.3 – in which improvements to the web browser will make pages load and render more quickly.

It has two cameras, both of which can shoot video as well as stills, has new gyroscopes to help it understand how it's being used and moved about, and comes with both black and white bezels and a choice of optional add-on covers.

Remarkably Apple has managed to do all of this without impacting either the battery life or the size of the device. iPad 2 still runs for 10 hours on a single charge – like the original – and is actually smaller than its predecessor by a not-inconsiderable 33%. It now tops out at 8.8mm at its thickest point.

By whichever metric you choose to use, iPad 2 is a remarkable feat of engineering, and it pitches an already high benchmark even further, giving Apple's competitors a truly formidable challenge.

Already devotees of the original iPad, we have quickly fallen in love with its replacement. In this book we want to share that love with you, highlighting the iPad 2's most exciting features, helping you choose the appropriate device for your needs and showing you how to get the best out of it once it's left its box.

More than that, though, we've also written a completely new reviews section where we highlight 30 pages of the best applications, eight pages of the best games, and six pages of the hottest hardware add-ons. We've also taken a long, hard look at the best office suites for this most portable of all portable computers, to prove that you really can do a productive day's work on something without a dedicated hardware keyboard.

iPad 2 is a remarkable, extraordinary device. Come with us as we explore both this latest and the original Apple tablet computer.

Nik Rawlinson

Contents

There's a whole world of exciting applications and add-ons for your iPad, web sites to visit, reference apps to interrogate and free content to download. We explore them all... and more. Here's where we've filed it all away.

Welcome to the iPad

The iPad is the most radical product Apple has ever produced. With different models to choose from, though, which one best suits your needs?

Everything iPad

The iPad is the hub of a whole world of add-ons and accessories, and even the latest editions aren't the peak of development, so what comes next?

iPad online

With a fast wireless connection or good 3G reception, your iPad will keep you in touch with the wider world wherever you happen to be. In this section we take a look at using your iPad with social networks, how to legally download free content, and the best iPad reference apps, many of which make use of its Internet connection to keep on top of the most up-to-date content.

iPad applications

From native apps to must-have downloads, we guide you through the software that enhances any iPad user's day-to-day experience, plus how to keep your kids safe with its built-in parental controls.

THE INDEPENDENT GUIDE TO THE
iPad 2

Meet the team

EDITOR Nik Rawlinson

ADVERTISING

020 7907 6000 Fax 020 7907 6600 *alex_skinner@dennis.co.uk*
ADVERTISING MANAGER Alexandra Skinner 020 7907 6623
MAGBOOK ACCOUNT MANAGER Katie Wood 020 7907 6689
MAGBOOK ACCOUNT EXECUTIVE Matt Wakefield 020 7907 6617
AD PRODUCTION EXEC Michael Hills 020 7907 6129
DIGITAL PRODUCTION MANAGER Nicky Baker 020 8907 6056
US ADVERTISING MANAGER Matthew Sullivan-Pond +1 646 717 9555 *matthew_sullivan@dennis.co.uk*

PUBLISHING AND MARKETING

020 7907 6000 Fax 020 7636 6122
PUBLISHER Paul Rayner 020 7907 6663
MAGBOOKS MANAGER Dharmesh Mistry 020 7907 6100
MARKETING MANAGER Emily Hodges 020 7907 6270

DENNIS PUBLISHING LTD

GROUP MANAGING DIRECTOR Ian Westwood
MANAGING DIRECTOR John Garewal
MANAGING DIRECTOR OF ADVERTISING Julian Lloyd-Evans
NEWSTRADE DIRECTOR David Barker
CHIEF OPERATING OFFICER Brett Reynolds
GROUP FINANCE DIRECTOR Ian Leggett
CHIEF EXECUTIVE James Tye
CHAIRMAN Felix Dennis

HOW TO CONTACT US

MAIL 30 Cleveland Street, London, W1T 4JD
EMAIL mailbox@macuser.co.uk
WEB *www.macuser.co.uk*
PHONE 020 7907 6000

LICENSING AND REPRINTS

Material in The Independent Guide to the iPad 2 may not be reproduced in any form without the publisher's written permission. It is available for licensing overseas. For details about international licensing contact Winnie Liesenfeld, +44 (0) 20 7907 6134, *winnie_liesenfeld@dennis.co.uk*

MAGBOOK

The 'MagBook' brand is a trademark of Dennis Publishing Ltd, 30 Cleveland Street, London W1T 4JD. Company registered in England. All material © Dennis Publishing Ltd, licensed by Felden 2011, and may not be reproduced in whole or part without the consent of the publishers. The Independent Guide to the iPad 2 is an independent journal, not affiliated with Apple Inc. 'Apple' and the Apple logo, 'Macintosh', 'Mac' and the Mac logo are all trademarks of Apple Inc.

Printed in England by BGP Print Ltd, Chaucer International Estate, Launton Road, Bicester OX6 7QZ

The Independent Guide to the iPad

Chapter 1
Welcome to the iPad

What is the iPad?

You've no doubt seen an iPad – at least in pictures if not in real life – but what lurks behind that smart, bright, touch-sensitive screen? Here are the key features of the iPad 2 and how it differs from its predecessor.

The visual differences between the original iPad and the iPad 2 are small. The most obvious is the fact that the iPad 2 is also available in white, whereas the original model, like the first Ford, was only available with a black bezel.

Look closer, though, and you'll see that iPad 2 is not only lighter – by up to 129g in some cases – but thinner, too. Apple has used its expertise in unibody design to slim down this remarkable device, effectively shaving off the walls of the old iPad so that only the curved back remains. This makes more of a difference than you might imagine as it has removed roughly a third of its depth, making it more portable and easier to hold.

Apple has also done away with the old black fold-over case that enveloped the old iPad, and instead produced the SmartCover (*see below*). These neat, colourful covers are held in place by

magnets and roll out of the way to form a triangular stand to support your iPad. They have a lined underside to clean your screen and, as the iPad can detect their presence, closing them puts it to sleep, while opening them up wakes it.

The biggest change under the hood is the processor, which has been bumped up from the original Apple A4 to the new A5. This is a dual-core chip, which has twice the resources to throw at the task of executing your applications. As a result they should launch more quickly and be more responsive in general use – including when you're using the multitasking features to switch between apps.

The graphics performance has been given a boost, too, with Apple claiming that iPad 2 is nine times faster when running games or video-intensive applications. This is good news for more demanding users who should enjoy better frame rates, and it

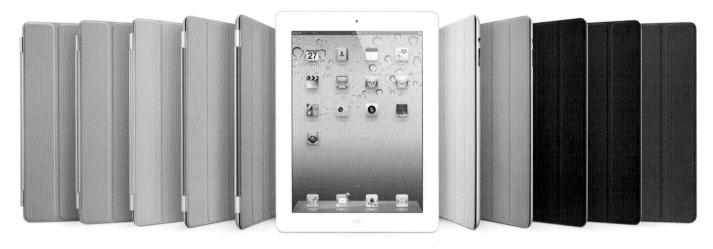

	iPad 1	iPad 2
Processor	1GHz Apple A4	1GHz Apple A5
Screen	9.7in / 1024 x 768 resolution / 132 pixels per inch	
Storage capacity	16GB / 32GB / 64GB	
Weight	680g – 730g	601g – 613g
Dimensions	241.2 x 185.7 x 13mm	241.2 x 185.7 x 8.8mm
Cameras	None	Front: 640 x 480 Back: 720p HD
Battery life	10 hours on one charge	
Sensors	Accelerometer Ambient light sensor	Accelerometer Ambient light sensor Three-axis gyro
Connectivity	wifi, Bluetooth, optional 3G, optional GPS (with 3G)	
Cellular compatibility	UMTS / HSDPA (850, 1900, 2100MHz) GSM / Edge (850, 900, 1800, 1900MHz)	
Audio features	Dual mono speakers, Bluetooth, 3.5mm stereo jack	
Operating system	iOS 4.2 and later	iOS 4.3 and later
Colour options	Black	Black or white
Announced	27 January 2010	2 March 2011

could really push the iPad fully into the realms of online multi-player gaming.

The screen resolution remains unchanged, perhaps so that Apple has something on which to sell the iPad 3, but just above it on the front there is now a forward-facing camera for using iOS 4.3's FaceTime and Photo Booth applications. This has a fairly conservative resolution of just 1024 x 768 pixels, but on the back of the device there is a second, far more ambitious snapper. This can shoot 720p high definition video, which can then be edited on the iPad itself in applications such as iMovie, which is a paid-for download from the App Store.

Whereas the original iPad came only with a black bezel, iPad 2 supplements this with a white option, from day one. Apple was keen to make clear the early availability of this colour option following delays to the iPhone equivalent caused by hold-ups in the manufacturing process.

iPad 1 and iPad 2 may look very similar – on a superficial level, at least – but when you look closely at the specs, and even more if you get to play with the two models side by side – you realise how much of an advance the second generation machine is. The fact that Apple has been able to maintain its original prices makes it all the more impressive.

10 reasons...
to buy yourself an iPad

Are you having difficulty justifying your purchase of an iPad? You've lived this long without one, after all, so why should the appearance of a smart new gadget from Apple mean you can't live a moment longer without splashing out?

If you need to justify to yourself – or indeed your partner, parents or children – why you should invest in an iPad for your own enjoyment, here are the top ten reasons for buying one of these sleek, beautiful, digital slates – or, indeed, for upgrading from the original model.

Battery life

If you're going to watch films without an interruption, you need to be sure that your battery won't run dry half way through. Tests and reviews have consistently shown that Apple's claims of around 10 hours' Internet-based use on a single charge are realistic. This is thanks in part to the low-drain components, but also to the smart, pared-down operating system under the hood that's been tailored to provide just the functions you need, without excess, in the most efficient way for the processor and surrounding hardware.

No network fees

With two models to choose from, Apple gives you the choice of a 3G or wifi-only iPad. While the wifi-only device won't be able to access the Internet, email and other online resources when you're away from your home or office network, the fact that you won't be signed up to a cellular provider means you won't be tied into an ongoing monthly contract. You can use all of the iPad's most innovative features for free on your own network.

Perfect for dummies

The iPad is a sealed unit. That means you don't need to worry about upgrading it over time or diagnosing problems with the operating system. Every application is vetted by Apple, so it remains virus- and glitch-free, and your computing experience will be smooth and easy.

Built-in applications

Unpack your iPad, switch it on and you're ready to go. The iPad comes preinstalled with a wide range of first class applications that will handle all of your most common tasks – email, browsing, organising your photos and so on – without you having to install or pay for any more software.

Easy software upgrades

But what about all those applications that don't come as standard? Well, you're sorted there, too, with the inclusion of the App Store on the iPad home screen. Apple has built itself a well-managed ecosystem that surrounds the iPhone, iPod and now iPad, with hundreds of third-party developers around the world working on software for these devices, ready to be installed automatically with one tap of your finger.

But what about Flash?

It is now a well-known fact that Apple has not authorised Adobe's Flash player for use on the iPad, iPhone or iPod touch. Flash is used by many online applications and games as a means of providing real-time interactivity. It is present on close to 100% of desktop and laptop computers. Apple would argue that it is not required on iOS devices such as the iPad because HTML5 provides many of the same features in a lighter, native way, and in many cases that's true, as can be seen in online applications such as MobileMe at *me.com* and Google Calendar. In practice, the absence of Flash on the iPad will impact very few users.

iPad-unique applications

Although the iPad will run every iPhone application, over 65,000 have been written purely for the iPad, to take advantage of its bigger screen and other dedicated features. That number includes Apple's own office suite, iWork, which has been ported from the Mac to the iPad. The component parts – Pages, Numbers and Keynote – could yet turn out to be the killer apps for the iPad, helping to push the device even further into the mainstream.

Dump your desktop Mac (or PC)

Thanks to its optional Dock with keyboard, you can use your iPad as a fully-fledged desktop computer. Because it is designed to sit in the stand in portrait orientation it offers a view of your work that isn't available to the regular computer user, who must spend more of their time scrolling their pages up and down to get an overview of their whole document. Third-party manufacturers have produced their own alternatives to the dedicated iPad keyboard, giving you a wider choice. Tap around a few of them until you find the one that's most comfortable for your way of typing.

With one of these sitting before it on the desk, and the iPad propped up so that you can easily see the screen, it can quickly become a work-anywhere device, allowing you to tap out notes on the train using the on-screen keyboard, and then switch to the desktop keyboard to finish your work when you get to the office.

Bright, big screen

If you want to watch movies on the move, you can squint at your iPhone or iPod touch, but imagine how much better it would be to enjoy them as Hollywood intended – on a bright, wide screen. The iPad's 9.7in display is perfect for on-the-move entertainment, helping your daily commute fly by.

A better iPhone experience

The iPad can do almost everything an iPhone can, with one crucial difference: it doesn't make calls. That isn't surprising, considering its size, but it does mean that all of your favourite iPhone features will be bigger and easier to use. If you have trouble typing on your iPhone, the iPad should solve that problem and your productivity should increase by an order of magnitude. Games, too, benefit from the bigger screen, giving you a better view of rendered scenes and more space in which to tap the controls.

The best of the web... made better

Think of the web's most innovative features, and improve on them. That's what Apple has done with the iPad. The dedicated YouTube application wraps up the web's best video sharing site in a fully-fledged interface, making it easier to search and enjoy user videos. Likewise, the Maps application simplifies Google Maps, letting you switch in an instant between plan and satellite views, and follow directions whatever your destination.

	16GB	32GB	64GB
wifi-only	£399	£479	£559
wifi and 3G	£499	£579	£659

eBay or which hemisphere you're standing in when looking at the stars.

By opting for one of the 3G models you'll be buying an iPad that can use data from the global positioning system (GPS) network to plot your location to within a few metres.

Size matters
Physically, it makes very little difference which model you choose. Whether or not you opt for 3G, your iPad 2 will be 241.2 x 185.7 x 8.8mm in size (height x width x depth). Adding 3G features will increase the weight by just 12g to 613g, which in day-to-day use will be barely noticeable. It will also add a plastic strip to the top of the rear panel to house the Sim. Otherwise, the two lines are identical.

A more meaningful 'size' measurement is your iPad's capacity. As you can see from the table above there are three capacities to choose from, with each step up double the size of its predecessor. Fortunately, with so many common components inside each one, doubling the capacity doesn't simultaneously double the price.

It's tempting to immediately opt for the highest capacity you can afford, but by thinking carefully about the way you'll use your iPad before splashing the cash you can save yourself a tidy sum, which you can then put towards some apps to run on it.

What does each one mean in real-world use? Most iOS applications are fairly small, and you could expect to fit around 50 average size downloads into just 5GB. Assuming a 4MB file size for a regular music file, even the 16GB model would give you enough space to store around 4,000 tracks – about 400 albums-worth – if you didn't use it for anything else. Most users could therefore afford to start by looking at the lower end of the scale and work up from there, and only consider the 32GB and 64GB models if they are sure they will be installing a lot of

games or copying videos from their Mac or PC for viewing on the move.

Do bear in mind, of course, that a small portion of the capacity of each iPad will be consumed by the operating system and default applications, such as Address Book, Mail and so on. In real world use, therefore, you won't have the full capacity available for your own use.

Refurbished iPads
Scroll down to the bottom of Apple's online store (*store.apple.com/uk*) and you'll find a link to its Refurb Store. For those in the know, this is a shopping gem. It offers significant discounts on current products, and you can often make a saving of up to 50% on some slightly older goods.

You shouldn't be shy to buy refurbished products direct from Apple, or from its authorised third-party resellers who often provide a similar service.

Any product bought from the Refurb Store – including iPads – will have been thoroughly checked over by Apple and will be supplied with a warranty, so you can return it for Apple to sort out should it develop any problems.

Refurbished goods are supplied with all of the add-ons that would have originally shipped with the product, including any necessary adaptors, cables, installation discs and instruction books.

First-generation iPad
Apple will continue to support the original iPad for the foreseeable future, but it won't continue to do so indefinitely.

iOS 4.3, the operating system update that shipped on the same day as iPad 2, was a free update for anyone using an original iPad and there is no indication from Apple yet that future editions won't also be available for the original model. If you're not too worried about the speed increases in both processor and graphics hardware that you'll enjoy when you buy iPad 2, you might therefore consider buying an original iPad.

This can deliver real cost savings. On the day it announced iPad 2, Apple immediately dropped the price of the original iPad by £100. Third-party resellers are likely to do the same, and this will continue until supplies are exhausted, at which point the second hand market will be the only legitimate channel through which to buy an original iPad.

Should you buy one? In the short term, the answer is yes. The original iPad remains a very capable device. It is thicker and slightly heavier than iPad 2, and it is also slower. It features the single-core A4 processor, rather than the dual-core A5 found in the iPad 2, so runs slower. It also has slower graphics processing, but if you're not going to play demanding games you probably won't notice too great a performance difference.

It also lacks iPad 2's gyroscopes, which are used by some applications, such as GarageBand, to register velocity so that the force with which you tap on the screen can affect the outcome – for example, banging a drum louder if you tap harder.

However, some owners of the original iPhone are starting to find that some applications don't work on their handsets. This is either because Apple is no longer shipping iOS updates for their device, meaning that applications that use the operating system's most advanced features are beyond their reach, or because the hardware is no longer up to

the job. This will happen with the iPad, too. As Apple ships ever more advanced units the chance of all applications working on the original iPad will get ever slimmer.

If you want to use FaceTime to communicate with friends and family then you should certainly *not* be looking at an original iPad. It doesn't have cameras on either the front or the back of its casing, so FaceTime is a definite no-no.

Which iPad is right for you?

If you have not yet bought an iPad, there are therefore several factors that you should consider. Answering the following three questions will help you rule out those that don't meet your requirements leaving you, hopefully, with the one iPad that perfectly suits your needs.

- Will you always (or almost always) have access to a wireless network? If so, you can save money by ruling out the 3G models. Unless...
- Will you be travelling away from home, in which case a 3G model with no contract may be a better option.
- Are you happy to take only a subsection of your music and videos with you? If so, opt for a cheaper, lower capacity and synchronise more often.

iPad vs Kindle

At first glance, Amazon's Kindle seems to be very much the poor relation when compared to the mighty iPad, but for the avid reader there are many areas in which it is the better choice.

One of the iPad's headline features is iBooks, Apple's own eBook reading application. It is tied to the iBook Store, through which 2500 publishing houses now sell their wares. Over the first nine months of operation, the Store shipped more than 100 million books, many of them free.

Apple was far from the first player in this field, though. Sony has long been shipping its own Reader device online and through bookshops, but perhaps the most important of all the rivals is the Amazon Kindle. The best-selling product of all time through Amazon's online store, the Kindle is slim, light and easy to use, and tied to one of the biggest online book catalogues in the world. No wonder it has been so popular. So is it a better choice for the avid bookworm?

Kindle facts

The Kindle isn't a full-blown tablet computer like the iPad. Its web browsing features and MP3 playback tools are 'experimental' and hived off into a secondary menu. It isn't backed up by a large App Store like the iPad and iPhone, and it doesn't have a colour screen.

The screen technology, though, may be a big factor in its success. Rather than LCD, as used by the iPad, which relies on shining light from behind the screen to illuminate the display, the Kindle uses electronic paper. This doesn't have any backlighting and relies on the ambient light that falls on to the reading surface from the front. This is much easier on the eye than the iPad display, but it does rely on having fairly good front illumination, which explains why Amazon also sells a case with a built-in light.

Kindle hardware

Like the iPad, Kindle lets you choose between wifi-only and wifi-and-3G models. Both are considerably cheaper than the iPad. They use these wireless connections to download books and synchronise your library across multiple devices, and to buy books direct from Amazon's online Kindle store. You can also connect by USB and transfer files manually by dragging and dropping them from your Mac or PC.

That's where the similarities to the iPad stop, though. The screen is smaller (6in, compared to the iPad's 9.7in), but because it's only displaying text and images rather than application interfaces this doesn't matter – it's more than enough for regular use. Neither is the screen touch-sensitive, so you use buttons set into the left and right edges of the device to turn pages back and forth, which flash as the page refreshes. You quickly stop noticing this flash, and it's quicker than turning a real page in a proper book. Amazon has made the buttons quieter in the latest line-up, so you won't disturb a sleeping partner when reading in bed. You might think this sounds somewhat old-fashioned when we're all getting used to the idea of touching, pinching and swiping on glass screens, but in use it works very well as it can be done with just one hand, holding

Unlike the iPad, the Kindle's screen doesn't have a backlight. It therefore relies on external light, just like a regular printed page. For this reason Amazon sells a range of illuminated cases for the device. Because the screen is not touch-sensitive it is not made of glass, so is not prone to reflections and less prone to glare than the iPad, making it better for use in bright sunlight.

and pressing at the same time. You can hold and tap the iPad with one hand, but it's not as easy as it is with the smaller, lighter Kindle, and so the Kindle is better-suited to commuting on trains so packed that you have to stand, while holding on to an overhead rail for support.

These page turners are far from the only buttons, though, as the Kindle also sports a full keyboard, which is used to interrogate the store and make notes, which can be synchronised and backed up online.

Kindle pricing and flexibility

The Kindle is cheap, starting at just £111 for the wifi edition and £152 for the 3G edition. Compare that to the iPad and you'll see that although you're getting a lot less functionality you're also paying a lot less for it.

Both the Kindle and Apple's iBooks app have their own stores, which significantly undercut the high street. Because digital books don't need to be stacked on expensive retail shelves and needn't be shipped around the world on boats, planes and trucks, publishers and the shops themselves can afford to pass on some of the savings to customers.

While the Kindle itself may be cheaper than the iPad, and so the best choice for anyone who will spend most of their time reading rather than using applications, Amazon has somewhat muddied the waters by producing Kindle applications for various

third-party devices, including the iPad. This means you can buy Kindle books without a Kindle device, thus benefitting from access to a wider range of stores if you use the iPad. However, precisely because of the existence of these applications, the Kindle may be better future-proofed, as you can transfer your books between devices as you upgrade or switch allegiances.

iPad v iPhone

Sure, they look similar, and the iPad can run iPhone apps, but that doesn't mean they have equivalent features. Ideally we'd each have both, but if you can't afford that, then the question is, which is the right choice for you?

The iPad is more than just a slimmed down iPhone (or, indeed, a slimmed-down iPod touch). Beyond the obvious size differences, there are significant differences to the way in which each one works and what they can do. How do you choose?

Communication

The big question is: do you need to make calls on your mobile device? If the answer is yes, then the iPad is not for you. Or, at least, the iPad alone is not for you. Why? Because while the iPad can come with or without 3G connectivity, it is only used for data transfer, not for voice calls or text messaging. That means you can use it for your email and browsing the web, but not for calls.

You can, however, run FaceTime. This is Apple's own video conferencing software, which lets you make calls using the built-in microphone and the front- and rear-mounted cameras over an active wifi network to other iPad 2, iPhone 4, iPod touch or Mac users. It doesn't work over 3G.

Productivity

Although there are several spreadsheet and word processing applications for the iPhone, Apple's iWork suite is perhaps the best iOS option.

Unfortunately it is written exclusively for the iPad and won't run on the iPhone or iPod touch. If you want a finger-driven device for working on the move without a mouse, track-pad or hardware keyboard, the iPad wins hands down against the iPhone.

Besides, the iPhone would be so small you have to ask whether you would be able to see well enough to do your work without a lot of panning.

The most remarkable thing about the iPhone, on launch, was how good the on-screen keyboard really is. If you haven't tried typing on an iPhone or iPod touch, visit your local Apple dealer and try it.

Now multiply that up to the scale of an iPad and you'll understand just how good the iPad is to type on. Its on-screen keyboard is almost the same size as a regular netbook keyboard and when the iPad is in landscape orientation it can occupy the full width of the screen. If your mobile working requires more than occasional typing, go iPad.

User Experience

What are you going to use your iPad for if not for working with words and numbers? Pictures? Movies? TV downloaded from the iTunes Store?

In all of these respects the iPad wins out. The 9.7in screen is perfect for watching videos without being so large that you're encroaching on the seat of the commuter beside you. It saves you from squinting and peering which, because you're holding it closer than you would sit to your television at home, gives you an experience far closer to what you're used to when you're watching movies from the comfort of your TV.

And when it comes to photos, the iPad is remarkably close to the size and shape of a picture frame, allowing you to show off your shots to friends

and family without everyone having to crowd around or pass the device from person to person. With iPad and iPad 2, photos are something you can enjoy communally again – just as you did when you last sat down with a box of slides.

With the inclusion of two cameras on the iPad 2, even capture is no differentiator. Previously the iPhone had a lead here, thanks to the two cameras found on opposite sides, but not any more.

Size and specs

The most obvious difference between the two devices is their physical size. The iPad 2, like its predecessor, is far larger than the iPhone. It's no bulkier, though. In fact, at 8.8mm in depth the iPad 2 is considerably slimmer than the iPhone 4, which is pretty impressive when you consider its increased footprint.

The larger screen, as we have already hinted, makes the iPad 2 far more usable than the iPhone for a whole host of applications. Even those that run on both platforms, such as iMovie or Scrabble, deliver a far better overall experience as you're covering up a smaller proportion of the screen with your finger each time you tap its touch-sensitive surface.

The iPad 2 also uses this additional space to cram in some impressive technology that's not present on the current generation iPhone.

The iPhone features the advanced A4 processor, which was designed in-house at Apple to drive its

portable music products. The same processor was found in the original iPad, but iPad 2 uses its successor – A5. This has two cores, so will perform many actions at twice the speed of the original. It also has an improved graphics engine, which can perform graphical functions up to nine times faster than its predecessor, making iPad 2 an excellent portable gaming device. The iPhone is good, but not that good.

The primary downside of all this additional real-estate is the loss of portability. You can easily carry around the iPad 2 on your day-to-day travels if you're happy to put it into a bag, but not if you want to leave that bag at home and slip your primary communications tool into your pocket. Here, the iPhone is the clear winner. It isn't much larger than a very plain calls-and-texts-only phone of a few years ago, yet boasts many of the features of a full-blown computer. Even when slipped into a case it doesn't grow to an unmanageable size. The iPad, on the other hand, even with just the SmartCover, which adds far less to its dimensions than Apple's own case for the original iPad did, would only fit into a set of unnaturally large coat pockets.

	iPhone 4	iPad 2
Processor	A4	A5
Size (h x w x d)	115.2 x 58.6 x 9.3mm	341.2 x 185.7 x 8.8mm
Weight	137g	601g (613g for 3G)
Screen size	3.5in	9.7in
Screen resolution	960 x 640 pixels	1024 x 768 pixels
Battery life	10 hours	10 hours
Capacity	16GB or 32GB	16GB, 32GB or 64GB

Which should you buy?

So what is right for you? An iPhone or an iPad? As ever, your choice should be determined not so much by bragging rights, but by what you want to do with your chosen device once you've handed over your money.

If your primary intention is to consume media, either online or locally on your chosen device, then the iPad is unquestionably the better choice. Its 9.7in screen is a luxury on a mobile device and it will let you enjoy your media to the fullest, either on your own or with family and friends.

If you're going to be creating rather than consuming, though, the choice is more to do with the kind of content you'll be creating. Documents? Go for the iPad. The applications that make up Apple's iWork office suite are among the most attractive business tools you can buy, and they work beautifully with the on-screen and optional external keyboards.

Extensive Microsoft Office compatibility from rivals such as Quickoffice Connect mean you really can create documents from scratch while you're away from your desk and continue working on them when you get back to your base.

In the previous edition of this book we had recommended the iPhone as the only option for taking photos, since the original iPad didn't have a camera. As has been much discussed since its appearance, the iPad 2 has remedied this situation, now sporting two cameras of its own, which allow it to take photos and shoot high-definition video. However, whether you would want to be taking many photos on something the size of an iPad is open to debate. The iPhone is close to the comfort limit already, despite being less than a quarter of the size of the iPad. With a larger footprint and a shallower depth, it may take a little bit of time before you're entirely happy about using it to take your own photos.

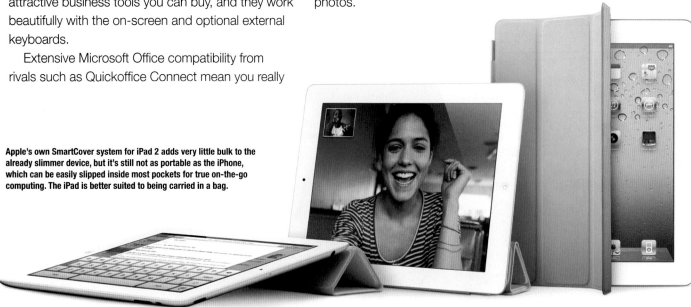

Apple's own SmartCover system for iPad 2 adds very little bulk to the already slimmer device, but it's still not as portable as the iPhone, which can be easily slipped inside most pockets for true on-the-go computing. The iPad is better suited to being carried in a bag.

Chapter 2
iPad applications

Native applications

Even if you chose not to buy any third-party applications, you would find plenty of high quality software installed on your iPad when you took it out of the box. Here's what you get for your money.

The iPad, like the iPhone and iPod touch, comes pre-loaded with a range of essential applications that help you keep in touch on the move, play your media, stay in touch with friends, family and business contacts, and control the way that the iPad works. Even if you never venture onto the App Store there's plenty to keep you busy.

COMMUNICATION

The iPad doesn't have any phone tools, perhaps because Apple doesn't want us all to think of it as little more than an oversized iPhone, but it does have three killer communications tools built in: Mail, Safari and FaceTime.

Safari

Safari (right) is available for the Mac, Windows, iPhone, iPod touch and iPad. It is one of the first five browsers to appear in Windows 7's browser election screen, which should mean that over time it becomes even more widely used. That's good news for all iPad users who will benefit from more widespread support from a broader range of sites.

The real benefit of browsing on the iPad, though, is that web sites are traditionally laid out in a vertical manner, with pages far longer than they are wide. By using the iPad in portrait orientation you'll be able to view pages from top to bottom with less scrolling and, if you want a wide view of the world, turning it through 90 degrees to landscape orientation will zoom the page to fit the width.

Mail

Mail (right) is one of the most attractive email applications on any platform, and being sensitive to the orientation of the iPad it will redraw its interface in one of two ways to make best use of the available space. Hold your iPad in portrait orientation and you'll give over the whole of the screen to just one message; turn it through 90 degrees and you'll see a more traditional email application layout.

Mail won't stumble on attachments. The most common file types are handled with aplomb, saving you from waiting until you get to a fully-featured desktop or laptop before you can open attached PDF documents, Word files, images and so on.

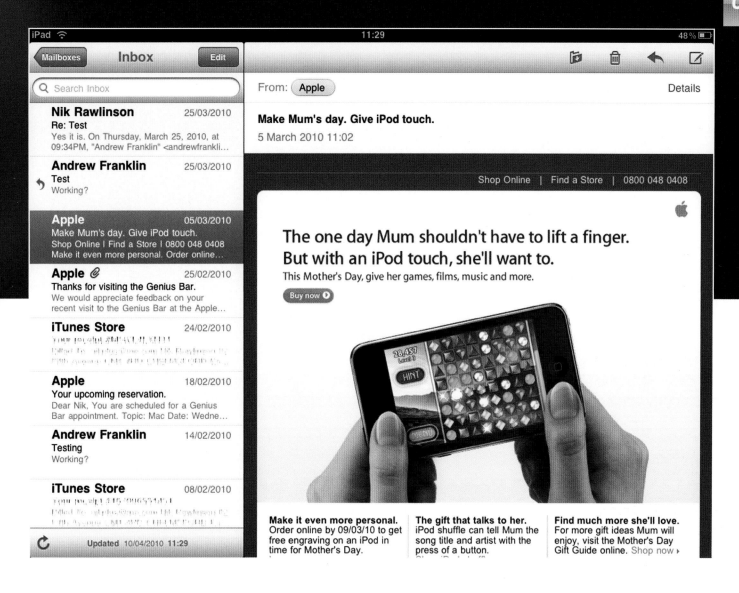

The iPad's Mail application will be instantly familiar to anyone who uses a Mac on a day to day basis as it is almost identical to the application of the same name that ships as a part of Mac OS X. It takes an already excellent application from the iPhone and, thanks to the bigger screen, makes it a joy to use.

FaceTime

Putting the front and rear cameras to good use, FaceTime is a wifi-based video calling system that lets you make Internet calls to friends and family with an iPhone 4, iPod touch, Mac or other iPad 2.

You use the front camera to address them directly, and can tap an icon to switch to the rear-mounted device to give them a view of what you can see behind the iPad. Best of all, all calls made on FaceTime are free.

MEDIA

The iPad has changed the way we consumer media for ever. With all the great features of iTunes and the iPod, and the added bonus of iBooks it is an end-to-end media playback device. Plus, with the option for publishers to create their own bespoke applications it looks set to become the vital shot in the arm required by newspaper and magazine publishers worldwide.

iPod

The iPod is the most successful portable media player of all time. In fact, it is so successful that Apple chose to name a piece of software after it: the iPod application on the iPhone. It's no surprise, then, that it now features in a bigger and better format on the iPad (see over).

No longer do you have to scroll through a list of tracks and artists, and neither do you have to flick through your album covers one by one in CoverFlow. Thanks to iPod on the iPad you can view your music library as a collection – just like you do at home. Whether you're using it in landscape or portrait mode, your album covers are presented in all their glory, while a category list on the left hand side, including Podcasts, Audiobooks and your own playlists, lets you navigate easily between different media types.

It has Genius built in, so can draw up on-the-fly playlists of tracks that go well together, so you'll always hear a fresh stream of music suited to your particular tastes. Songs are loaded onto your iPad through iTunes, either on your Mac or PC, or on the iPad itself. Tracks you buy directly from the iTunes

Store on the iPad will be synchronised back to your computer the next time you connect by USB.

iTunes

iTunes is your window on the iTunes Store, giving you access to an unrivalled collection of music and movies. Unlike the Mac- and PC-based version, it isn't a playback application. It is also the tool that will manage how and where you access your downloads, synchronising what you have bought between the iPad and your main computer every time you dock the two.

YouTube

YouTube is the web's best-known movie sharing site, and the YouTube application (right) built into the iPad builds on its success. Rather than presenting you with a view of the site in its native format, it wraps it up in an attractive interface, helping you to find related content whenever you finish watching an uploaded video.

Because of the size of its screen you can also watch higher-definition videos in their best possible quality, so for any YouTube addicts who spend a lot of time watching posted movies on their iPhone or iPod touch, this one feature could well be enough to justify the cost of upgrading to the iPad on its own.

Videos

If you've ever watched a video on an iPhone or iPod, you'll know what it feels like to wish you have some extra space. In that case, the iPad may be the answer to your wishes. You can buy films and TV shows directly on the iPad through the iTunes Store or synchronise them to the device from iTunes on your Mac or PC. When you have done so, you can skip straight to specific points and navigate to chapters, just like you can with a DVD.

The iPad's battery really comes into its own here, allowing you to watch up to 10 hours of video on the go, so no matter how delayed your commute might be, you probably won't want the journey to end.

Photos

The iPad gives you simply the best photo viewing experience, bar none. It's easy to get your photos from a Mac or PC onto the device and, once they're there, show them off to family and friends. iPad 2 can now take its own photos, and Apple also makes two adaptors: one for connecting your camera directly to the iPad, and one for inserting a media card.

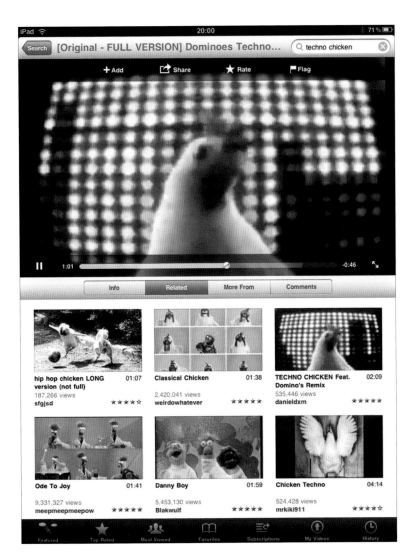

The Photos application arranges your shots in stacks which, when tapped, open up to show the pictures each one contains. With a 9.7in screen in your hands you have a bigger viewing window than is presented by most digital photo frames, so it's not surprising that it's great for gathering around and looking at your photos.

Photo Booth

Photo Booth first appeared on the Mac where it used the built-in iSight camera to present a live view of the person sitting before it, which could then be manipulated in a number of amusing ways, warping and twisting the image.

Thanks not only to its cameras but also its dual core processor and impressive graphics performance, the iPad 2 can now do the same, presenting nine live streams that you can manipulate at will, actually moving the point of distortion in real time by dragging it with your finger. It's a bit of fun, of course, but one that actually works better on the iPad than its native Mac edition.

PRODUCTIVITY

The iPad is more than a cool media player. It's also a fully-fledged business and productivity device, as evidenced by the fact that Apple has rewritten its Pages, Numbers and Keynote office tools to run on its smaller screen. They are charged-for downloads and don't come pre-installed, but four essential business tools will appear on your home screen from day one.

Calendar

Calendar applications are among the oldest uses of personal digital assistants, of which the iPad is the ultimate evolutionary point. Its built-in calendar application is arguably the best portable day book since the Filofax, with daily, weekly, monthly and list views and a beautiful interface that mimics regular paper-based diaries and spiral-bound calendars, depending on your orientation and view (above).

The application's name is slightly misleading, because it's not one single calendar, but a whole host of them, each colour coded so they can be displayed simultaneously, without you getting confused about which appointment relates to which.

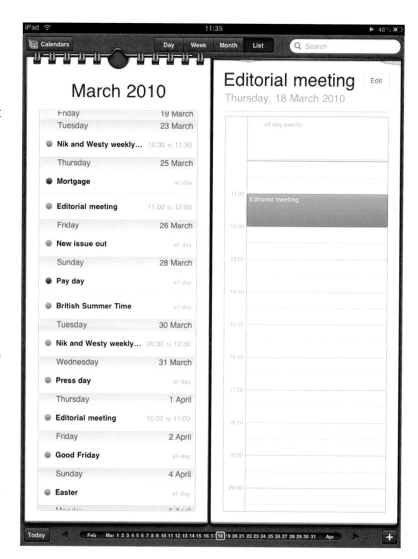

Contacts

The iPad is a great emailing device, which allows you to keep in touch with your friends, family and business associated wherever you happen to be. The Mail application is therefore backed up by a comprehensive address book called Contacts.

This opens like a traditional address book, with an indexed list of names on the left-hand side, and each of your contacts on the right. This right-hand page is highly reminiscent of the Mac OS X Address Book, and it can organise multiple email addresses and phone numbers for each contact, a generous clutch of notes, and even a photo to help you visualise them when you're composing a message in your head. You can also add birthday reminders that will appear in the Calendar application's birthday calendar if you have it active.

Contacts can be searched either from within the application itself, or using the Spotlight tool, which

where you are. Thanks to your iPad's built-in GPS receiver, the data from which can be combined with triangulation data from the mobile phone network and the IP details of connected wifi networks, Maps can show you exactly where you are, whether you are using the street view or satellite images. Once you know that, you can start to use its intelligent search tools.

These could be as commonplace as directions that plot the best route between where you are and where you want to go, or as complex as a series of map pins showing the nearest petrol stations, doctors' offices, pizza houses or branches of Starbucks.

With an iPad and the Maps application you really can throw away your atlas, which is out of date almost as soon as it's printed anyway, and with Safari waiting in the wings you can chuck out your guidebook, too. Lightweight 21st century travelling starts here.

Notes

You don't need to wait for a 'killer application' to justify the iPad: Apple has already provided it by porting its successful iWork suite of word processing, spreadsheeting and presentation tools to the platform. Sadly they aren't installed by default, and must be bought separately. However, that's not to say that you can't use the iPad as a writing tool as the basic but capable Notes application goes some way to plugging the gap.

Notes first appeared on the iPhone and then, on launch, the iPod touch. It looks like an American legal jotter with ruled yellow pages bound at the top, and with a margin running down the left-hand edge. When you type onto them your words appear in a marker pen font that looks like very neat handwriting.

You can keep as many notes as you like, and although they aren't well organised (they appear in reverse order of creation, with the most recent at the top) you can search their contents either within the Notes application itself or using the system-wide Spotlight search tool.

Notes is one of the iPad's native applications whose interface changes as you rotate the device. Hold your iPad in portrait orientation and the page takes over the whole screen, with a Notes button in

will drag in information from every application on your iPad, making it easy for you to see not only a contact's address and phone details, but also any email threads shared between you.

Records can be organised into groups, allowing you to keep all of your work, club and personal contacts separate and scroll through each one quickly without the clutter in each of the others.

Maps

You must be online to use the Maps application as it draws its data from Google's map servers. This is no real hardship as it means you can view not only a street plan but also high resolution satellite imagery (above), which looks so much better on the iPad's larger screen than it does on a poky iPhone or iPod touch display.

Maps is more than a digital atlas, though: it's also a constantly-updated guidebook that knows exactly the top left hand corner that, when tapped, drops down a list of pages in your notepad. Turn it through 90 degrees and hold it in landscape orientation, however, and you'll see that your notepad appears in an attractive leather folder with a pocket to the left, inside of which a slip of paper shows a list of your notes.

Four buttons at the foot of the notepaper let you flick back and forth through the pages, bin the note you're working on or send it via email using Mail.

SYSTEM

Apple thinks it knows how your iPad should be configured, but perhaps you have other ideas. The three core system applications installed natively on every iPad let you make the device easier to use, more functional with downloaded applications, and easier to navigate thanks to a powerful internal search engine.

Accessibility

The Accessibility application, found through the Settings app, lets you switch audio from stereo to mono, speak corrections every time it automatically changes your input, invert the display for improved legibility, zoom in on particular areas, and announce the elements that your fingers pass over.

Further accessibility features found in other applications that ship with the iPad include a screen reader and closed captioning (subtitles) for digital media playback.

App Store

Let's face it: the iPad's native applications are great, but the novelty would soon wear off if they were the start and end of all you could do with your new gadget. That was the case with the iPhone when it was first launched and Apple announced that if anyone wanted to develop apps for it they would have to do so through the browser. There was a minor backlash and, when buyers started to unlock their iPhones so that they could install whatever they wanted, Apple's hand was forced. It released a software development kit so that commercial coders could finally develop for the platform.

A variation on that development kit works on the iPad, allowing those same developers to retool their apps to take advantage of the iPad's bigger screen,

ArtStudio for iPad - Photography

and even if they should choose not to do so, native iPhone apps will run on the device. This is good news, as it means that on launch day the iPad already had access to around 150,000 third-party applications, each of which is downloaded from the integrated App Store. Now there are 65,000 iPad-optimised apps, too.

You can manage your downloads through iTunes on your Mac or PC, or directly from your iPad. Both let you search through the full catalogue and pay for downloads without using your credit card, whose details are accessed using a unique Apple ID.

The App Store icon is dynamic. It doesn't just give you access to the application itself, but also tells you about the state of your iPad, notifying you when updates are available for programs you have downloaded in the past by applying a small badge to the upper right corner containing a digit showing the number of updates waiting to be downloaded.

Spotlight

Spotlight is Mac OS X's search tool. It finally appeared on the iPhone and iPod touch with the version 3.0 software update. Now it appears on the iPad, too, and is accessed by swiping the home screens all the way to the left.

Spotlight loves to search, and it doesn't care where it's looking. Start typing in its input box and it immediately heads off around your iPad gathering up matching information – everything from notes and contacts to appointments and messages sitting in your inbox. As you keep typing, it keeps searching so that while it might pull up a lot of contacts and incoming emails as you type 'dan', they could well disappear when you type another three letters to complete the word 'danger'.

This saves you the responsibility of keeping track of where you have filed your data. You simply need to do your work and be creative, and leave the filing up to your iPad and Spotlight, which appears both as its own application and as a tool in applications like Mail.

And... iBooks

Eagle-eyed readers will spot that this is almost the same name as Apple gave to its range of low-end portable computers. The iBook is now long-gone, but the company has recycled the name for an application on the iPad.

iBooks downloads reading matter from the online iBookstore and also lets you add your own books in ePub format from your computer. It's a beautiful electronic book reading application with crisply-rendered text and full colour images.

This is clearly Apple's riposte to the Kindle, which Amazon is hoping will turn us all on to digital, rather than paper-based reading, and in some (but not all) respects the experience is superior. The most obvious difference is the colour screen. Some users may be put off by the shiny surface when comparing it directly to the Kindle's matt surface, which is the price you pay for colour. Check out page 18 for our comparison of the two devices.

iBooks is not installed on the iPad by default. In the countries in which Apple has signed agreements to distribute books through the iBookstore, the application is a free download from the App Store.

There's more...

Over the next 85 pages, we'll take a closer look at the most compelling native iPad applications, before going on to show you how you can download and install your own. In the next section, we'll pick the best apps available from the Store.

By the time we get to the end, you will see just how flexible this remarkable device is, thanks to the tireless and ever-expanding community of developers working to write software for you.

Mail

The iPad is one enormous step up from the iPhone when it comes to handling your email. Here we take a look at its most prominent features and how you can put it to best use.

Email is one of the most important tools for any mobile worker. Rim discovered that when it released the Blackberry, which offered its owners always-on email access wherever they were. The Blackberry was a smash hit, for both business and home users. Apple followed suit with the email application in the iPhone and iPod touch, and now it's done the same with the iPad, with a first-class email application that really makes the best use of the 9.7in screen's available space.

Hold it horizontally and you will see a split screen, with either your folders or the contents of your selected mailbox in the left-hand column (below). The main part of the screen, to the right of this, is where the content of your email will be, whether you are reading or writing.

Open a mailbox by tapping on it, and the top of the message list will sport a useful search box,

allowing you to hunt through your messages for particular content, without having to open up each one individually.

If you turn the iPad to portrait mode, the screen looks quite different. The whole display spins around, with the static mailboxes or message list swivelling off the left hand side, and a new toolbar appearing at the top of the screen. This has the same controls for filing, deleting and forwarding a message at the right hand side, alongside the new message button on the far right, but to the left it now also has an inbox button and up and down controls. These controls step forwards and backwards through messages (see far right).

The inbox button is of most use, as tapping it drops down a list of your incoming messages, allowing you to skip straight to the one you need without stepping through those that appear around it. It also reinstates the search box.

However you display the inbox contents, whether as a permanent panel running down the screen beside your message body of in this floating overlay, you will see an Edit button at the top. This button is key to controlling the contents of your mailbox and maintaining a proper filing system.

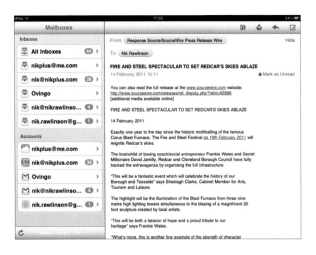

The mail application's versatile interface makes excellent use of the device's 9.7in screen (see left). It may not have as much room to breathe as a Mac- or PC-based email client, but by subtly swapping our various display elements depending on the task you are performing at any particular time. Here we are sitting at the top level of the interface, with our mailboxes on display. Tapping the accounts in the top half of the column takes us straight to the inbox for each one, but tapping those that appear in the Accounts section, below, displays the folders inside each one.

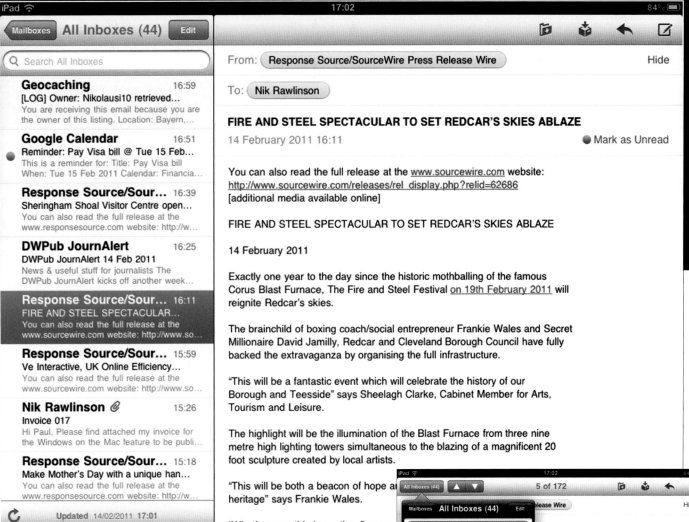

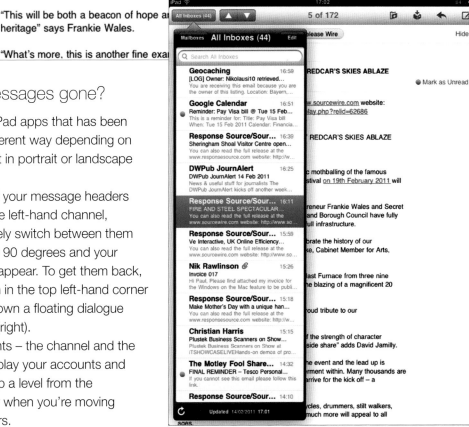

Where have my messages gone?

Mail is one of the native iPad apps that has been designed to work in a different way depending on whether you are holding it in portrait or landscape orientation.

Hold it horizontally and your message headers will always be visible in the left-hand channel, allowing you to immediately switch between them (above). Turn it around by 90 degrees and your message headers will disappear. To get them back, tap the All Inboxes button in the top left-hand corner of the interface to drop down a floating dialogue showing your messages (right).

These interface elements – the channel and the drop-down – will also display your accounts and inboxes when you step up a level from the messages themselves, or when you're moving messages between folders.

How to delete multiple messages

There are two ways to delete single messages from your inbox. You can either tap the trash icon on the menu bar or, if that's not present, swipe a single finger across the message header in the inbox listing in the left-hand column to call up the Delete or Archive button (see below).

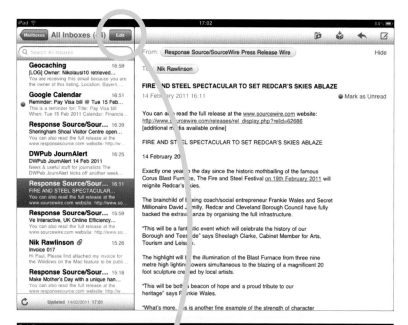

This isn't a practical solution if you need to delete a lot of emails at once, though, as it would take you far too long to step through each one. Fortunately, though, there is a simple way to delete several messages at once.

Look at the top of your message list for the Edit button (step back into your inbox if you can only see the list of your mailboxes in the left-hand column).

Tap the button and all of your messages will shift to the right to make space for a column of lozenges. As you tap each one – and you can tap more than one in sequence – you will select the message beside it. You can then delete the selected messages by tapping the red delete button.

Notice how every message that you have selected to delete is stacked up in the right-hand window so that you can preview it before wiping it from your iPad. If you change your mind about removing one from your mailbox, tap its lozenge in the left-hand panel for a second time to clear it, and it will be removed from the deletion stack. This works even if the message is not displayed on the top of the stacked queue.

If you don't want to delete the messages, but instead move them to another mailbox, tap the Move button at the bottom of the column and you will be returned to the overall mailbox view. Here, tap on the mailbox into which you want to move the selected messages. See the tip opposite for a quicker way to move just one message at a time between mailboxes on your iPad.

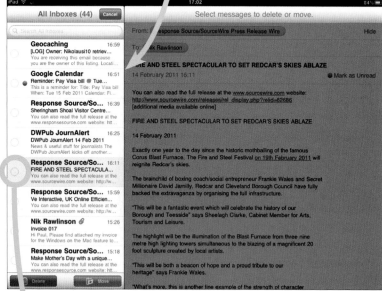

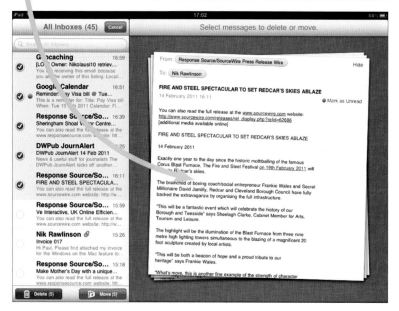

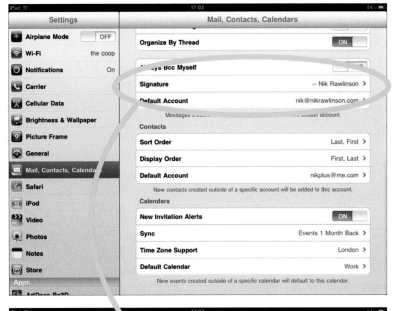

How to set up a signature

Save yourself some time by setting an automatic signature to appear on the bottom of each of your emails. This isn't done through the Mail application itself, but through Settings.

Tap Mail, Contacts, Calendars and scroll down to Signature (left). Tap this and set your signature in the box that appears, finally tapping the left-pointing arrow above it when you have finished.

TIP Add two hyphens and a space on a blank line above whatever signature you choose, as we have done in the image to the left. Why? Because when people reply to your email their email application will strip out your signature to save passing superfluous data backwards and forwards with each new entry in the conversation thread of messages.

How to move messages

When you've read an email, you'll often want to file it in a more appropriate folder than  your inbox. Rather than waiting until you're back at your Mac or PC, do it from your iPad. Tap the first icon in the buttons at the right of the toolbar (the folder with the down-pointing arrow on it) and the message will shrink to the middle of the screen. Your folders appear in a channel on the left. Select the one to which you want to send the message.

If you need to move it to another account, tap the Accounts button at the top of the list (see below), select the account you need and, again, choose the relevant folder.

The iPad keyboard

It may initially look a little too slimmed-down, but the iPad keyboard is actually highly versatile. Tap the .?123 button to either side of the keyboard, and then #+= to pull up the keyboard's extended character set. The keyboard icon in the lower-right corner hides the keys themselves to give over the whole of your screen to the body of your email.

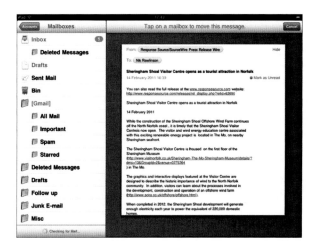

Safari

Apple's web browser now appears on no less than three platforms: the Mac, Windows and iOS devices. Here's how it works on your iPad, and how to save shortcuts to the home screen.

Safari is the iPad's web browser. By default it is found on the Dock so that it appears on every home screen – that's how important it is.

If you use Safari on the Mac or PC, many of its controls and interface elements will already look familiar. The toolbar that runs across the top of the screen has your forward and back controls, a button for opening new browser windows, the bookmark manager (it looks like an open book) and the shortcut saver (the box with an arrow coming out of it) and then two input boxes: the address box, where you type the address of the page you want to visit, and the search box, where you enter terms that you want to send to Google.

This mobile edition of Safari is more intelligent than a general desktop or laptop browser, as it knows a lot more about the dimensions of the page you are browsing. Turn it to portrait or landscape orientation and you'll see that it resizes the content to fit the width of the screen, allowing you to choose between a wider, larger display, or a taller display that shows you more of every page. It also knows the dimensions of everything on the page so that double-tapping any element, such as a column of text, zooms the content until that element takes up the whole width of the screen, whichever way up you have it.

All of Safari's controls are clustered on the toolbar, with many of the buttons sporting drop-down dialogues that reveal hidden features. Tap on the address box and start typing in the URL of the page

you want, and a list of matching addresses you have recently visited will drop down so you can pick the one you want without typing the whole address. Likewise, start typing in the search box and it will drop down a list of suggestions from Google and, below the list, any searches you have recently performed that match what you have typed so far.

The bookmarks button (the open book icon) drops down a list of your set bookmarks, at the top of which you'll see an entry for History. This, logically, lists all of your recently-visited pages, divided by date so that if you recall visiting a particular page last Monday you can skip straight to it. They are arranged by date, with your most recently-visited pages at the top of the list, and older history items filed into chronological folders.

That leaves us only the screens button. This is the icon showing two overlaid rectangles. Tapping it calls up a list of all of the open pages currently active on your iPad, with a space at the end of the list for another new page. The iPad's multi-page features are limited to nine pages at any one time. When you reach this limit, the New Page space will disappear.

Shortcuts
Save a page to your bookmarks, or create a shortcut for your iPad home screen and save yourself some future typing.

Reload
Click the circular arrow to refresh the page, or to reload it entirely if your iPad had problems downloading it the first time around.

Bookmark / History
Want to keep track of your current page for your next session? Save it as a bookmark or find it in your history through this button.

Screens
Safari can open up to nine pages at once on the iPad. Click this button for an overview of your active page thumbnails.

How to manage your shortcuts

However good the iPad's on-screen keyboard may be, you don't want to have to type in the address of every page each time you start Safari. For that reason you might want to save your favourites as bookmarks (see facing page) and shortcuts.

Shortcuts are a great feature that take you straight to a page from an icon on the iPad home screen, without you needing to manually invoke Safari in the first place.

To place a shortcut on your home screen, fire up Safari and visit the page you need (don't worry – this is the last time you'll have to start the browser yourself).

Tap the shortcut button to the left of the address box. It's a rectangle with an arrow flying out of it. From here you can save a bookmark, email a link to the page, print it to a compatible printer or, of most interest to us, add the page to the home screen. This last one is the option you're after. Tap it to create your shortcut.

Safari will suggest a name for the shortcut, based on the text that appears in the browser title bar. This will most likely be a description of the content rather than the name of the site itself, which the publishers of the site have used to optimise its performance in search engines like Google. Delete the contents of the name box and enter your own. Here, we have chosen *The Guardian*, as that's the site we're saving to the home screen.

When you tap the Add button, your shortcut will be created and dropped into the first available space on your home screens. It will take whichever icon has been set by the site owners.

Tapping this icon will now take you straight to the site, making this an excellent way to access app-like sites such as Gmail and Google Reader. However, you might either tire of the site or find something better in the future, at which point you'll want to remove the shortcut.

Hold down you finger on any icon on your iPad's home screen and wait until all of the icons start to shiver. Each one will be overlaid by a small 'x' in a circle. Tap this and you will be asked to confirm that you want to delete the shortcut. If you do, tap Delete and it will be removed. Tapping Cancel leaves it in place. When you have deleted all the links you need, press the iPad home button to exit.

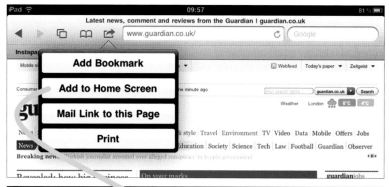

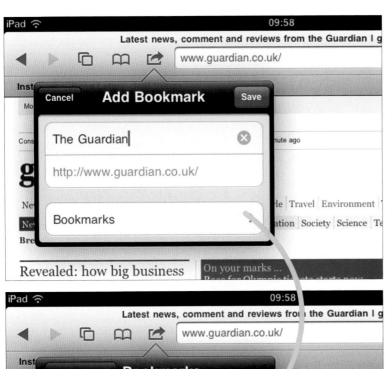

How to save a bookmark

Even if you don't want to create a shortcut for each of your favourite pages, you can still bookmark them to make them easy to find later on. Once again, start by visiting the page you want to save and then tap the shortcut button. This time tap the Add Bookmark button.

Again, Safari will suggest a name for the bookmark but you can change this before going on to choose where it is saved. By default it will be saved in your bookmarks folder, but if you will be accessing the page particularly regularly then you might instead want to save it to the Bookmarks Bar, which appears below the address box and gives you one-tap access to your favourite sites. To do this, tap Bookmarks at the bottom of the floating dialogue box and then Bookmarks Bar in the new dialogue. Tap Add Bookmark to complete the process.

The desktop version of Safari lets you drag links straight off the Bookmarks Bar, at which point they disappear in a cloud of smoke. You can't do that on the iPad, but you can still delete them. Tap the Bookmarks button (the open book to the left of the shortcut button) and then tap the Bookmarks Bar within it. This will display all of your existing links. Swipe to the right across the one you want to delete and then tap the red Delete button that appears.

How to use Safari's live search

You can't change the default search engine in the mobile edition of Safari the way you can in a regular desktop browser. It's set to Google, which should suit most users as it's the most commonly-used search engine anyway, and it also has a very neat predictive searching feature.

Start typing in the search box to the right of the address bar, and you'll see that your current page dims and suggestions for what might be searching for appear in a drop-down dialogue, which extends from the bottom of the search box.

The longer you type, the more accurate the suggestions become as Safari automatically retrieves a refined list from Google. If it comes up with the answer you're looking for, tap it. If not, tap Search as usual to visit the Google results listing.

Maps

Who needs an atlas when you've got an iPad? The built in maps tool not only displays global street plans – it also helps you get around by car, bus and foot.

Maps is one of the many iPad tools that relies on third-party services to answer your queries. In this instance, that service is Google's online Maps, which you can access through a browser at *maps. google.co.uk*.

The Google Maps web site presents highly accurate plan maps and satellite views of the world. You can switch between them and zoom in or out to get a closer look or a more distant overview of an area. You can do the same on the iPad. Tap the curled-up corner in the lower-right of the interface and you'll expose the view menu, which lets you switch between views and turn on or off the traffic overlay. This overlay marks up roads on the map in green, amber and red depending on the state of the traffic so that you can make a decision whether or not to follow a particular route depending on road conditions.

The more you zoom in on the map, the more detail you will see, and as with other applications on the iPad, you zoom in and out by pinching and reverse pinching the screen. You scroll by dragging your finger across the surface, and to quickly locate yourself on the map, tap the compass arrow icon on the toolbar. This sits beside the address book icon, which lets you tap a contact's name to have the location of their associated address pinpointed on the map.

Maps is more than just a digital atlas, though. It is also a local gazetteer. Find your local area and then search for a business – say a pizza restaurant. Type pizza in the search box and map pins will drop down to locate local pizza houses in your area. Tap each one to call up their names and when you find the one you want tap the arrow icon at the end of each name. This brings up contact details, including phone numbers and addresses, and options to plot a route either to or from that restaurant.

You can tailor your directions depending on your mode of transport, with options for car, public transport and walking. Each one will be drawn along the shortest appropriate route for that means of travelling, along with estimates of the journey duration. Once you have chosen the means of travel you want to use, click Start and the iPad Maps application will take you step by step, turn by turn, through each leg of your journey.

If you decide to take public transport, then be sure to tap the clock icon on the blue information bar. This calls up public transport timetables, so takes care of all of your planning for you. By default it will display the next two or three departures. If you don't want to travel right away, choosing a later time is simply a matter of tapping the Depart box at the top of the panel and choosing a different time and date, at which point the directions will update.

Unfortunately, in the UK at least, public transport directions are confined to use on foot and bus as our test journeys involving well-known railway commuter routes took convoluted paths along major road networks. Nonetheless, for local travel it is hard to beat.

How to choose different map types

Maps can display four different kinds of map, depending on your needs. Each is provided by Google, and you can switch between them by tapping on the curled up corner in the lower-right of the application. This reveals a menu containing links to the classic map, a photographic satellite view and a terrain view that marks out hills and valleys in 2D using shadows and highlights.

There is also a hybrid option, which combines the classic and satellite views to overlay a traditional drawn map on top of photographic satellite imagery to clearly mark out the names of roads.

The option to switch on traffic is only relevant in certain parts of the world. There is fair coverage around major UK cities, where roads will be colour-coded green, amber or red, depending on the weight and speed of traffic using them.

How to find your home on Maps

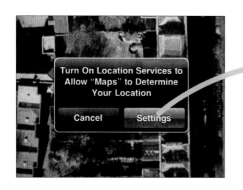

Tap the arrow icon on the Maps toolbar at the top of the screen. If you haven't enabled Location Services for this application you'll see this pop-up warning. Tap Settings to switch it on.

You'll be sent to Settings where the Location Services page will be opened. Look for Maps in the list and tap the slider to move it from OFF across to ON.

Return to the Maps app and a blue pointer will drop on your location. It may initially wander as it gets an accurate fix on your home. The blue circle shows its margin of error.

How to plan a journey with Maps

Maps isn't just about street plans. Double-tap a location on the map and then tap the blue arrow on the pin that appears and you can use that as a start point for mapping a route. Choose whether you want directions to or from that location and then type your origin or destination, as appropriate, in the empty box on the toolbar.

Maps pulls up the quickest route by road between your two points and tells you both the distance and the time it will take. If you'd rather go by foot or by public transport, tap the pedestrian and bus icons on the blue bar at the bottom.

The public transport option links in to timetables, so tapping the clock face icon on the bar pulls up a list of the next available departures that would get you to your chosen destination.

If you aren't planning on travelling immediately, tap Depart at the top of the floating dialogue and you can specify whether you want to set a time to leave or the time by which you must arrive.

With this done, use the barrels to select a date, hour and minutes, and then tap Done to confirm.

With your journey now fully defined, by whichever mode of transport, tap Start on the blue bar to set off, and use the forwards and backwards arrows that appear to navigate each step of the way.

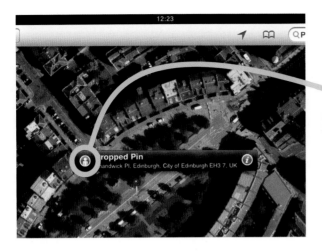

How to use Street View

Google Street view lets you look at a road at ground level. Switch from the regular overhead view by tapping the orange circle on any dropped pin or address, and then navigate the roads by tapping the arrow in the direction you want to travel. Drag your finger on the screen to turn yourself around.

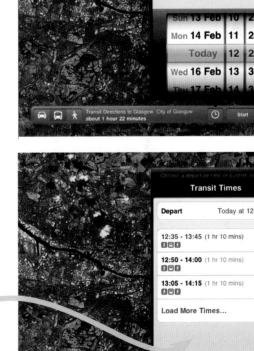

iPod

The device that revived Apple's fortunes may have been the original iMac, but it was the iPod that put it into overdrive. Now it appears in software form on the iPad, too.

Don't confuse the iPod and iTunes applications. On your desktop or laptop computer, you'd use iTunes to listen to your music, but on the iPad (and iPod touch and iPhone) it's only used for downloading content. The iPod application is where you'll turn to listen to your music and watch videos.

Despite this, iPod bears more than a passing resemblance to iTunes on a regular computer. The interface is split into two, with library categories running down the left-hand side in a panel of their own, and albums displayed to the right. If you have relevant artwork for all of your albums, they will be displayed like albums on a shelf, or books in the iBooks application. Dragging your finger up and down on the screen scrolls through the albums in your collection.

Below the albums are buttons that let you change the main display to sort your content by song name, artist name, album, genre or composer. All of the data attached to your tracks that makes this possible is transferred at the same time as your music if you are filling your iPad from a Mac or PC, or downloaded at the same time as your purchases if you are buying content from the iTunes Store.

The easiest way to find a track is to use the search box. As you type, it will trim the list of results in the window below. It also greys out some of the buttons at the bottom of the screen to leave only those categories your results appear. The longer you type, the more of these will disappear, but if you still have more than one in full black text, you can tap

between them to filter out those items that don't meet your requirements.

Although the library looks quite sparse when you first start using iPod on the iPad, you can build it up by creating playlists in which to organise your tracks. Tap the '+' at the bottom of the display and enter a name for your playlist then, to populate it, tap the elements you want to include. Again, use the category buttons at the bottom of the screen to switch between artists, albums and so on, selecting tracks from each one. When picking tracks from an album, tap the album's cover art and it will flip over to show you a track listing, from which you can select the tracks you want to include.

If you don't have the time or the inclination to build your own playlist, then why not ask your iPad to do it for you. Beside the playlist '+' button you'll see what looks like some neutrons spinning around each other. This is the Genius button. Genius builds playlists of tracks that go well together based on information submitted anonymously by the millions of iTunes users around the world. Tap it and select a starting track, and iPod on the iPad will build a playlist of 25 songs that it thinks go well together. If you don't like them, tap Refresh or, if you think they're perfect, opt for Save.

The iPad's built-in speaker is fine for system sounds like alerts and alarms, but might fall short when listening to music unless you're using headphones, or speakers connected to your network using AirPlay.

iPad 📶   11:32   48% 🔋

0:28

Library

 Music

 **Podcasts**

 **Audiobooks**

 **iTunes U**

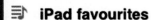 **iPad favourites**

Progress
As you play each track, this spot will move along the channel to show how far you are through. You can rewind or fast forward using the buttons above, or hold your finger on the spot itself and drag it in either direction to skip straight to a specific point.

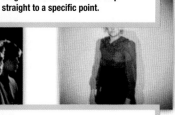
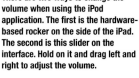

Aerial
Kate Bush

Atomic: The Ver...
Blondie

...ea...

Volume control
There are two ways to change the volume when using the iPod application. The first is the hardware-based rocker on the side of the iPad. The second is this slider on the interface. Hold on it and drag left and right to adjust the volume.

Confessions On A...
Madonna

Dangerously In Love
Beyoncé

The Division Bell
Pink Floyd

Playlists
These categories organise the content of your iPod library into logical, easy to understand groupings. You can create your own playlists either inside iTunes on your Mac or PC, or on the iPad itself. To do this, tap the '+' at the bottom of this left-hand channel.

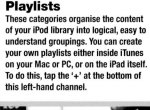

Fleet Foxes
Fleet Foxes

Headlines And Deadl...
a-ha

The Hits/The B-Sides
Prince

Artwork
Every track you download from the iTunes Store is accompanied by cover art, and for those that you have ripped yourself you can add your own scanned files. They are used in the library listing, seen in the background, and in the Now Playing panel here.

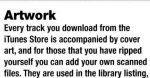

▶ **Kylie Live In New York**
Kylie Minogue

Live at Hammersmith...
Kate Bush

A Long Dream About...
Tyler Ramsey

Now Playing:

Kylie Minogue
Speakerphone (Live In New Yo...
Kylie Live In New York

Minor Earth Major Sky

Nine Objects Of...

Genius
iPod's Genius feature examines the music in your library to find tracks that work well together because they have complimentary stylings and beats. Tapping the Genius button creates a bespoke playlist containing these complimentary tunes.

\+

Songs   Artists   Albums   Genres   Composers

How to build a playlist

Playlists let you gather together a collection of your favourite tracks, or tracks of a certain type, such as Christmas music, and organise them in one sorted list so that you can always get to them without having to skip backwards and forward through individual entries in your library.

Start by tapping the '+' button at the bottom left of the iPod window to create a new playlist, and give it a meaningful name.

As soon as you tap Save, iPad hides the sidebar so you can concentrate on adding tracks to your freshly created playlist.

Use the buttons at the bottom of the screen to switch between songs, artists, albums, genres and composers as you build up a list of your favourite tracks (and they needn't only be songs).

You can use the search box at the top of the screen to narrow down the list of tracks from which you can choose, and the list below it will be thinned as appropriate. Once you've found the tracks you're after, tap each one and it will be added to the playlist, at the same time being greyed out in the listing to that you know it has already been selected and needn't be added twice.

When working with albums you're shown a library of covers, with each one comprising the fronted by cover art from the iTunes Store or your PC- or Mac-based iTunes Library.

Tap an album you know to contain tracks you want to use and the artwork will flip over and enlarge to display a scrollable list of the tracks on that album on the back. Again, tap the ones you want to add to your playlist.

To remove tracks from a playlist, open the playlist from the sidebar and tap the Edit button at the top of the screen, then use the red '-' buttons beside each one.

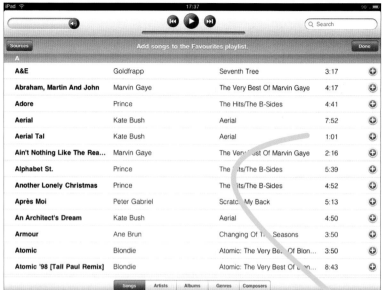

How to explore your albums

You might not think the album view is particularly informative, showing only a grid of your imported or downloaded albums, but it is actually a great piece of design, allowing you to quickly glance across your library to get a feel for what's available, and then tap your chosen album to flip it around and see the tracks that it contains. Each one is listed in order, with a track number, name and length, and the currently playing track – if it appears on the selected album – is marked out with a small play triangle.

To step out of the track listing and return to the album overview screen, tap the grey title bar, or anywhere on the screen away from the tracks.

How to enjoy your cover art

It seems such a shame when you have a glorious 9.7in screen at your disposal to only ever view your album art in the grid view, or as a thumbnail in the bottom left corner of the screen when you're playing a track. Tap that thumbnail and the album art expands to fill the whole screen. Tapping it again overlays it with various playback controls. At the top of the screen are the volume, play, forwards and backwards buttons. Below these, the progress bar and, to the left and right respectively, the repeat and shuffle selectors. At the bottom of the screen you'll see three buttons: return to the playlist on the left, build a genius playlist in the centre, and a button to flip over the artwork and display the album tracks.

How to build a genius playlist

If you don't want to follow our instructions for building a defined playlist (see opposite page) you can assign the task to the iPod app. Tap the genius button at the bottom of the interface and then select a track from your library. Your iPad will examine all of the other tracks in your collection and pick out a list of other tracks that it considers work well alongside it. To do this it uses information submitted anonymously by the millions of iPod and iTunes users around the world, which is analysed centrally and accessed by the iTunes and iPod applications. As well as the current track you can see which tracks the iPod app has queued, allowing you to skip straight to a favourite entry.

The iPad App Store

The App Store is your gateway to a whole host of exciting add-ons for your wonderful iPad, but how do you use it? Here, we guide you through the process of buying your first downloaded application.

Installing applications directly on your iPad lets you add to its capabilities when you're away from your home or office and unable to attach it to your regular Mac or PC.

It is no more difficult than installing through iTunes and it uses the same login details, as it's tied to your iTunes Store account. This means that you don't need to store any valuable credit card details in a portable device that you may misplace when you're out and about.

Better still, when you return to your regular computer and next plug in your iPad to sync it, the exchange of data works in both directions, so apps that you have downloaded direct to the iPad will be backed up in your iTunes library.

The main difference between the way the process works on your regular computer and your iPad is that on the iPad you use the App Store application

from the Home Screen rather than accessing applications through iTunes, which on this platform is only used for buying music and videos.

The App Store has two tabs, allowing you to see what's new and what's popular. If you know what you're after you can safely skip both of these and start typing into the search box on the toolbar (see left). As you type, the App Store will suggest results. So typing weather, for example, will call up a list of applications that have that word in their title.

When you've found the application you want to install, click its entry in the results list and you'll be presented with a dedicated app page showing you example screen grabs and a short description of its features and capabilities. You can also see how other users have rated it and, crucially, what operating system it requires to work with your device. Over time Apple will likely issue updates that won't be compatible with all iPads, so this information will become more relevant.

If you want to purchase the application, tap the price or 'Free' beneath its icon at the top of the page and you'll see that it changes to read 'Install App'. This is the confirmation button: only tap it if you're happy to commit to buying and installing the application on your iPad.

Once you've tapped it you will leave the App Store (it will keep your place in the background so that next time you re-enter you'll find yourself back at the same page) and install the app, with a progress bar overlaid on its icon showing progress.

iPad 📶   09:16   100% 🔋

| New | What's Hot | 🔍 bbc news |

In the Spotlight

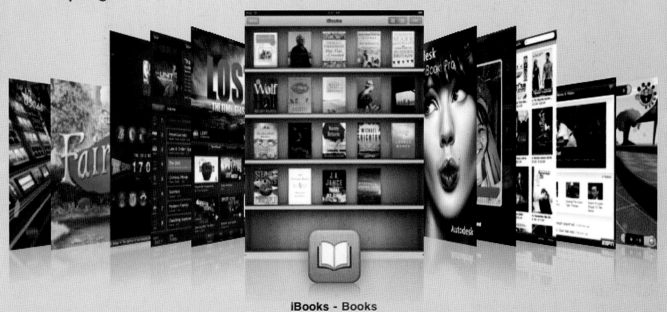

iBooks - Books

New and Noteworthy   See All >

◄   ● ● ● ●   ►

At Bat 2010 for iPad
Sports
Released Apr 01, 2010
★★★★☆ 156 Ratings $14.99

Evernote
Productivity
Released Jul 11, 2008
★★★★☆ 711 Ratings   ⊕FREE

Miss Spider's Tea Party for th...
Books
Released Apr 02, 2010
★★★★★ 9 Ratings $9.99

Gilt for iPad
Lifestyle
Released Apr 01, 2010
★★☆☆☆ 632 Ratings   FREE

Shazam for iPad
Music
Released Apr 01, 2010
★★★☆☆ 245 Ratings   FREE

KAYAK Flights
Travel
Released Apr 01, 2010
★★★★☆ 167 Ratings   FREE

◄   ● ● ● ●   ►

⊕ indicates an app designed for both iPhone and iPad

iWork for iPad

Featured   Top Charts   Categories   Updates

How to install applications, step by step

1. Tap the app's icon in the App Store overview to open its dedicated page. This includes a slideshow of images and a brief description.

2. The More... link at the end of the description opens a more extensive write-up from the app's publisher. This usually details its pertinent features, alongside details of what has been updated in the most recent version.

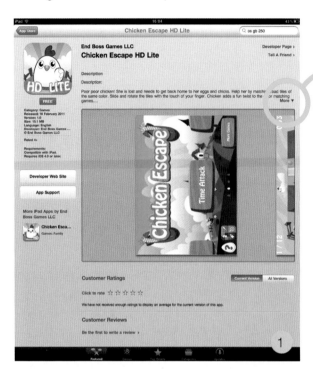

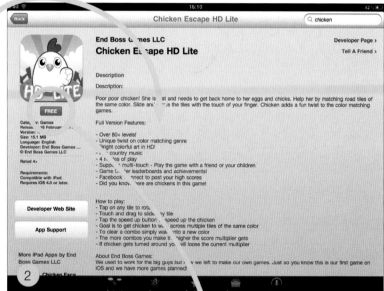

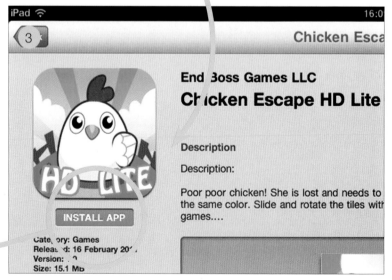

4. If you haven't installed any new apps or updates in the last few minutes, you'll be asked to confirm your password. This is to make sure that nobody is making unauthorised purchases on your account. You will receive an emailed receipt for all purchases that you do action a few days after you install them, with several totted up on a single invoice.

3. If you still want to download the app, click the button below its icon twice. This will read either FREE, or its price in the first instance, but tapping it for a second time changes these words to confirm that you want to install it.

How to keep your applications up to date

The iPad's active developer community is filled with enthusiastic coders who work tirelessly to keep their applications up to date, regularly shipping refreshed editions through the App Store. These updates are free to download, and you'll be notified when they are ready for you. Keep an eye on the App Store's icon on your iPad's home screen. When updates are ready it'll be overlaid by a small red badge, in the middle of which a number will tell you how many updates are ready to be shipped.

Open the App Store and tap the Updates icon at the end of the toolbar (again, this will have a badge attached, telling you how many updates are ready). This opens a page showing you what the updates are (1). You can install them one by one by tapping the button beside each one, or update all at once by tapping Update All at the top of the screen.

As your apps install their icon (2) or the folder holding them (3) will adopt a progress bar showing you how long you still have to wait.

The New tab shows you the latest popular additions to the Store. This is the place to look for featured new applications that you probably won't have seen before.

What's Hot shows you what people are downloading. Combine your investigations here with the Top Charts, accessible from the toolbar at the bottom of the interface.

Only interested in the very newest additions to the App Store? Tap Release Date to see which apps have just been released for sale and stay ahead of the crowd.

iBooks

The future of reading is almost certainly digital, and if Apple has any say in it, the device through which you'll do that reading is the iPad or iPhone, using the iBooks application. What is it?

iBooks is an important application for the iPad. Apple is hoping that the iPad will become a book replacement, and that we'll choose to read books on a screen – Apple's screen – rather than bound paper. It's not the first company to have this idea, as the likes of Sony (with the Reader) and Amazon (with the Kindle) already have competing products.

It's surprising, then, that iBooks isn't installed by default on the iPad. Instead, you have to download it for free from the iTunes App Store and, when it's installed, download the books you want to read.

Your books are arranged on shelves, a little like the albums in the iPod application. Tapping one opens it on the screen, either as a spread showing both the left and right pages on a landscape-oriented iPad, or as a single page on a portrait-oriented iPad. Which you choose is up to you, but if your only reason for using it in portrait mode is that you can read it more easily because the text is larger then you may want to increase the font size.

This is managed through the font setting dialogue that hides behind the AA button at the top of each page (see right). Tap this and choose between smaller and larger characters in five common fonts. The button beside it – the picture of the sun – controls the brightness of the display so that you can tailor it to your own particular eyes and the lighting conditions in which you're using your iPad.

To the right of both of these is a picture of a magnifying glass, which signifies the search tool (opposite page). Tap this and enter your search term

and it will hunt through the book you're reading to find every instance of that word combination. If it remains ambiguous, Google and Wikipedia buttons at the bottom of the results panel let you search online for more information.

Each time you open a book, iBooks will remember where you left it last time, so you shouldn't ever lose your place, and if you're on the contents page of a book you'll see a red resume tab at the top of the page that, when tapped, takes you to your last-opened page. However, you can also set bookmarks throughout the text. This feature will be particularly useful for academic texts. Hold down on a word where you want to set the bookmark and

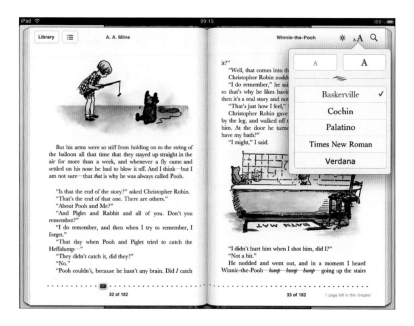

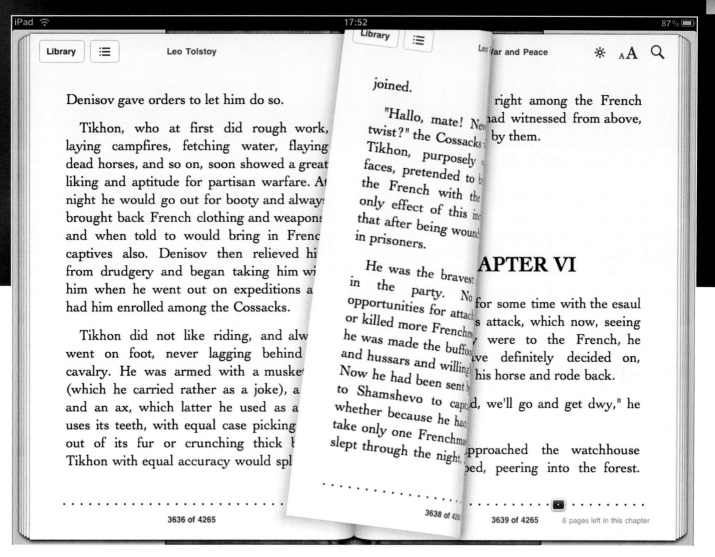

when you lift your finger you'll be presented with a short menu that lets you copy the selected text, use it as a search term, look it up in the dictionary or set a bookmark (below). Select the last of these options and the location will be saved in your bookmarks list, along with an excerpt and the date so that you

can easily find it in the future. The longer you use iBooks, the more you'll fall in love with this way of reading, with a progress bar at the bottom of the screen showing how far through the book you have read, and the integrated dictionary ensuring you are never lost in a sea of unfamiliar words.

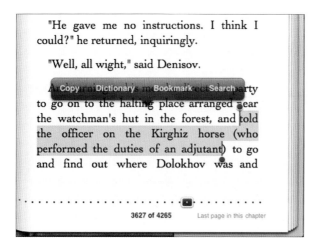

How to buy a novel in iBooks

Tap iBooks' Store button to flip around the application like a secret passageway hidden behind a bookcase. On the back you'll find a store that closely resembles the App Store. Tap Top Charts to see what's selling well right now, and which are the most popular free books.

Enjoying the book? Tap Buy to add the rest of it to your library.

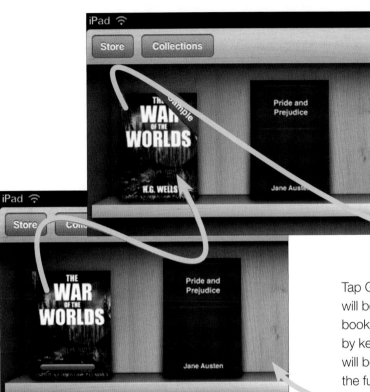

Tap Get Sample and a generous excerpt of your chosen book will be download to your iPad and deposited on your bookshelves. You can monitor the progress of the download by keeping an eye on the blue bar. When it has completed it will be strapped by the word 'SAMPLE' so you know it's not the full book. Tap the cover to take a look inside.

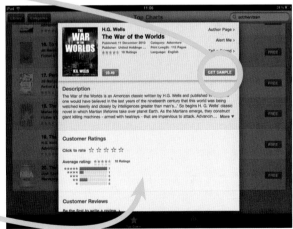

Scroll through the charts to find a book that grabs your interest. There are plenty to choose from, in all genres, but if nothing here takes your fancy use the search box at the top to hunt out a particular read.

Every full book is accompanied by an excerpt, which is free to download. This is the digital equivalent of flicking through a book in the shelves in you local bookshop, as it allows you to try it out before you buy the whole thing. The length of the excerpt varies between books, but should always be enough to give you a flavour of the full download.

iWork for iPad

iWork is Apple's consumer-friendly office suite, comprising a first-class word processor, spreadsheet and presentation tool. It's long been a joy to use on the Mac, and it's been a part of the iPad, too, since the very beginning.

iWork is Apple's own office suite, and it elevates this desirable gadget to the status of legitimate business device, despite having no hardware keyboard.

iWork

iWork has appeared in parts over the last few years as Apple first introduced presentation tool Keynote, then word processor Pages, and finally Numbers, its innovative spreadsheet. The iPad editions will be familiar to anyone who has used iWork on the Mac, but have been rebuilt from the ground up to take advantage of the iPad's unique way of working.

Although iWork maintains its own file formats, the three apps can also read and write industry standards. All can output PDF documents; Numbers exports Excel files and Pages will save in Word format. All can also make use of Apple's online *iwork.com* service for collaborative working.

Each of the constituent applications is available individually, so if you don't ever make presentations or work on spreadsheets, for example, you can just buy Pages and work on your words. This is in contrast to the Mac edition of the suite, which comes as a boxed bundle.

Pages

Pages is a word processor with a difference: it can also act as a low-end desktop publishing tool for laying out multi-column documents that mix text and graphics. As a purely finger-driven device, Pages takes much of the pain out of layout, allowing you to drag images and other objects around the page simply by pointing to them on the screen and sliding your finger. Try doing that on the Mac or PC and you'll see how much easier the iPad can be.

It will work perfectly well with the iPad's large on-screen keyboard, on which the keys are almost the same size as the ones you'd find on a regular laptop keyboard, but will really fly if you invest in the optional Dock with integrated keyboard or a separate Bluetooth keyboard so that you can stand up your iPad like a screen.

Depending on how you choose to work, you can hide many of Pages' on-screen interface elements so that there is less to distract you from your work.

Numbers

Nobody could see how Apple might improve on the tried and tested spreadsheet model when it released Numbers on the Mac, but it did. Instead of presenting the user with a single large table on each tab of their spreadsheet, taking up the whole page, Apple had the idea of using multiple discrete tables on each one. Not only is this logical, allowing you to sectionalise related sums while keeping them away from unrelated data that you nonetheless want displayed on the same screen, but it also means you can lay out your spreadsheet documents more clearly and attractively. When you're presenting numerical data – and particularly financial data – clarity is important for getting your message across quickly and accurately.

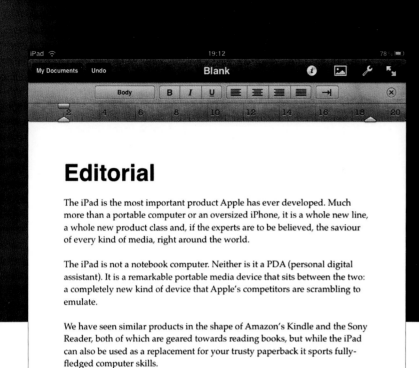

Editorial

The iPad is the most important product Apple has ever developed. Much more than a portable computer or an oversized iPhone, it is a whole new line, a whole new product class and, if the experts are to be believed, the saviour of every kind of media, right around the world.

The iPad is not a notebook computer. Neither is it a PDA (personal digital assistant). It is a remarkable portable media device that sits between the two: a completely new kind of device that Apple's competitors are scrambling to emulate.

We have seen similar products in the shape of Amazon's Kindle and the Sony Reader, both of which are geared towards reading books, but while the iPad can also be used as a replacement for your trusty paperback it sports fully-fledged computer skills.

With a generous bundle of native applications, to which you can add hundreds more by downloading them from the iTunes App Store. The most impressive among them are Apple's own iWork applications that give the iPad powerful word processing, spreadsheet and presentation tools.

Presentation is just as important in the iPad edition of Numbers as it is on the Mac, which is why, like the other iWork applications, it ships with a range of pre-defined templates – 16 in this instance – which guarantee a professional finished product.

Special cell types allow you to use your iPad as a sophisticated clipboard for data gathering, so you can design forms for filling out on the spot, with the collected data fed directly into a spreadsheet. This saves you from filling out a paper form when you're away from your work and transcribing the results when you get back.

Keynote

Keynote is Apple's presentation tool, roughly equivalent to PowerPoint in Microsoft Office. It's named after the presentations given by Apple CEO Steve Jobs whenever the company launches a new product.

If you've ever put together a screen-based presentation before, you'll find the tools in Keynote immediately familiar, with a slide organiser running down one side of the screen and a main area for designing slides to the right. Slides contain backgrounds, images and words, and you can apply a range of transitions that define how the application moves your presentation from one slide to the next.

Keynote for iPad ships with a choice of 12 Apple-designed themes, each of which contains a range of page templates that can be organised in whichever order you choose. It hooks in to the iPad's photos application, allowing you to draw in images from your library, and you can share data with other iWork apps, so if you need a table or a chart you can create it using Numbers and then import it directly. Over the pages that follow, we'll examine each app in more detail.

Pages

It may be unfamiliar to PC users, but Pages is a hit on the Mac. Now it's made the transition to the iPad, where it provides not only writing tools, but rudimentary page layout features, too.

Pages is a very accomplished word processor, giving you fine-grained control over the look of your work, with multiple fonts and the kind of layout options you might expect to find on the desktop.

It works well with the iPad's screen-based keyboard, but really flies when you marry it with an external keyboard – either by Bluetooth or using the Dock-connected keyboard that Apple sells as an optional extra. Dock it in portrait orientation and you'll have access to the formatting toolbar that runs across the top of the screen, with a comfortable, tactile keyboard below.

Pages is more than a simple text input application, though – it also has some pretty impressive layout tools at its disposal.

The toolbar button sporting the framed mountain view is the media button. This gives you access to your iPad photo library so that you can insert

pictures into your documents, and also tools for creating tables, charts and shapes with which to illustrate your work (see below left).

Impressively, for a device that doesn't have a mouse attached, once these elements are placed on your pages you have a lot of control over the way that they look. Place a photo, for example, and you can drag it around the page and watch as your text re-flows around it. It will be positioned within a frame with grab handles at the corners. Dragging these with your finger changes the shape of the borderless box in which it sits, while double-tapping the graphic itself gives you access to a resizing tool. This is a simple slider that enlarges your picture when dragged to the right and makes it smaller when dragged to the left.

Pages has been written to work with other applications. The My Documents button at the top of the screen calls up a gallery of the text files you have created, and tools for creating new ones, emailing those that already exist or exporting them in one of three formats: Pages, PDF and Word for using on a Mac or PC. This way you can use the mobile edition of Pages when you're away from home or the office in the confidence that you will have no problem continuing work on the same document when you return to base.

If you have signed up to Apple's online MobileMe service, you can also save your documents to its *iwork.com* site for reading and review by your colleagues and contacts.

Project Proposal

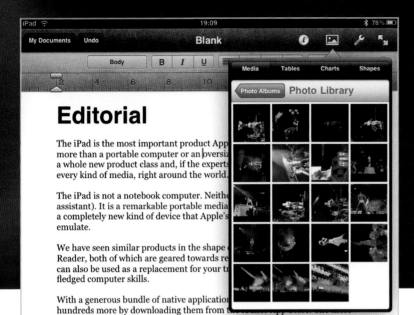

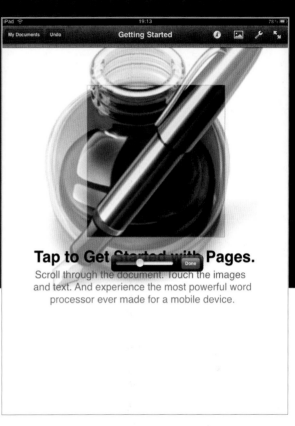

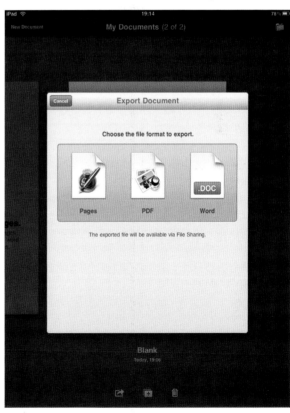

The many views of Pages

Above: The general editing view is dominated by your writing space. To the top of the screen is the formatting toolbar and ruler, both which can be hidden from view if you find them distracting. You can also hide the darker bar, which is where you need to look when you want to insert shapes and images or skip out of the editing view and back to the document organiser.

Above right: Despite being a tablet-based word processor controlled by nothing more sophisticated than your fingers, Pages lets you perform surprisingly advanced editing tasks, including resizing images. We're doing that here using an overlaid slider dialogue.

Right: Although Pages has a preference for its own proprietary format, which works with Pages on the Mac, PC users and anyone who wants to share their documents will want to export in a different format. Pages for iPad can happily handle Word and PDF output, both of which enjoy wide industry support.

Keynote

Anyone who has to present for a living understands the importance of a good set of slides. With Keynote you can build your own on the move, even if your Mac or PC has been safely left back at the office.

Keynote is Apple's presentation tool – its version of Microsoft's own PowerPoint. Unlike the other iPad iWork applications it only works one way around: landscape. That's because its content – the slides that you create – are designed to be shown on a regular computer monitor.

Well aware that not everybody is a skilled designer, Apple has included 12 high quality templates with the application. This is fewer than you'll find in the regular Mac-based version of Keynote, but if you're familiar with the desktop / laptop edition you will find that a number of familiar favourites have nonetheless made the transition to this mobile variant, including Chalkboard, Modern Portfolio and Showroom.

When you're building your presentation, the interface is split into two, with a channel for organising your slides on the left, and a larger area for the actual design of your slides to the right.

Apple has thought very carefully about the way that you would create slides without the use of a mouse, and has made everything easy to drive with the finger. A '+' button at the bottom of the organiser channel lets you add new slides, and tapping it will bring up a list of the different slide variations in your theme. Tap the one you want and it appears in the organiser channel.

Editing the slides themselves is just as easy. Tapping in a text area calls up the keyboard, allowing you to type directly onto the slide with full access to formatting and bullets. You can also change the way that your text appears on the screen for greater impact.

Again many of the familiar options from Keynote's Mac edition are present here, including Blast, Appear and Compress. You can tweak the speed at which the build completes and whether it happens manually ('On Tap') or automatically ('After Transition') in each instance.

Photos – for what is a presentation without its images? – are pulled in from your Photo Albums and can be resized on the slide itself. You can zoom in to a precise level and then pull the edges of the constraining frame towards the centre or edges of your slide so that the image is properly cropped. You can also apply effects such as concave and convex curls and simple drop shadows.

The iPad screen is an excellent medium on which to showcase your presentation, and if you buy the optional VGA or HDMI connection kit you can hook it up to a regular monitor or a projector for showing to larger groups. If you would rather show it on your Mac or a PC you can export it – as you can with the files created in Pages and Numbers. Sadly for PC users, you can't export your work as a PowerPoint .ppt or .pptx file, but only Keynote or PDF format, which really means that if you don't have a Mac with Keynote you must use PDF.

The iPad version of Keynote is among the most versatile and accomplished slide-design tools we have seen on any platform – not just on a mobile device.

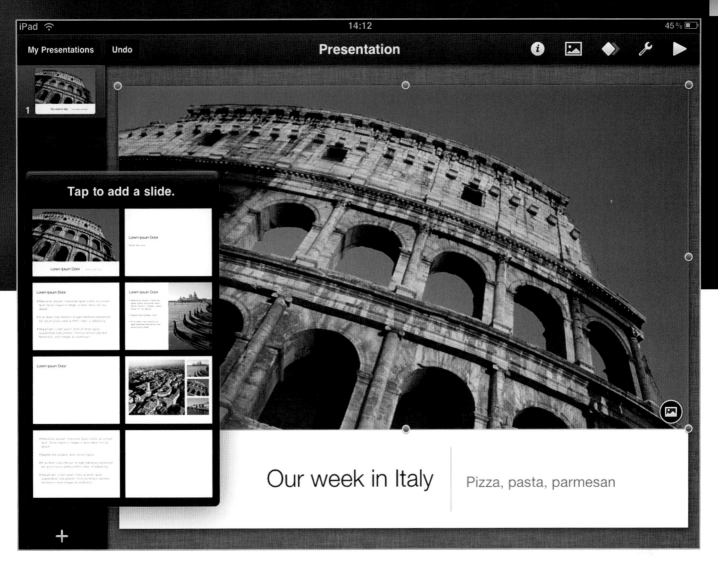

Top: Every theme in Keynote's arsenal features several different slide styles.
Left: Built-in tools let you tweak the way your images appear on screen, with a slider changing each one's size in its bounding frame.
Above: Lacking inspiration? Leap off with a pre-formatted template.

Numbers

Numbers is a sophisticated spreadsheet with great graphing tools to help you get a grip on your financial situation. It also had four rather clever keyboards that greatly ease the task of entering data.

If you have used Numbers on the Mac, you will know what a revolutionary piece of software it is. It completely rethinks the way that spreadsheets work, giving you access to several tables on a single sheet, rather than just several sheets in a single document, each with only one table.

Numbers ships with 16 different templates that take a lot of the hard work out of starting a new spreadsheet. Together, they cover every base, with pre-designed sheets for organising teams, invoicing and submitting expense reports, among others.

The most useful probably remains the blank table that presents you with an empty page. Crucially, this doesn't occupy the whole sheet in your document, but only a portion of it. Tapping it calls up handles at the bottom and right-hand edge which, when dragged, enlarge or reduce the size of the table on the sheet. Tabs across the top of the screen let you add new sheets to the document, each of which can contain several other tables.

To enter data you start by double-clicking on a cell. This calls up the familiar entry bar that you'll know from Excel or Numbers on a regular computer. Crucially, though, you will find it supplemented by four buttons to the left. These are for entering numbers, time and date, text, and equations.

Tapping through them, you will see that each one changes the keyboard that appears below the entry box. If spreadsheets aren't your strong point, there is plenty of help to be had through each one. Open the equations entry field, for example, and click on

Functions to call up a list of the commands that Numbers understands, from the fairly simple SUM, used to add, multiply, subtract and so on, to more complex IF functions that test conditions within cells in your spreadsheet and act upon their findings.

As with Pages and Keynote, you can incorporate other media into your documents, including photos, shapes and graphs drawn up using the data in tables on your various spreadsheet pages. Graphs are easily tailored by dragging your finger across the cells in your tables to set the range to be displayed within them, while cycling through the various pages in the Charts panel of the media drop-down box lets you choose the colour scheme used to illustrate each one.

Cells can be formatted en masse or individually by tapping or drag-selecting and then tapping the 'i' button on the toolbar. This opens up a menu from which you can choose common data types, such as numbers, currency, percentages and so on. More interestingly, though, you can also insert check boxes into cells in your spreadsheet that can be ticked and unticked using the digits 1 and 0, and star ratings of the kind you find on the iTunes Store that are set using the numbers 0 to 5.

Like Pages and Keynote, Numbers has export options for sharing your work with other applications. Available export formats include Numbers, which will only be of use to anyone with Numbers on a Mac, alongside Excel .xls for Mac and PCs and the almost universal PDF format.

Above: Numbers isn't all about digits and decimal points. Its sophisticated graphing tools help you illustrate what your workings mean in a more engaging and immediately understandable way. There's a wide range of graph types to choose from, with one for every situation.

Below: With four specialised keyboards that you can switch between at will, Numbers greatly eases the task of entering almost any kind of data. These keyboards are one of the features that make this perhaps the most versatile spreadsheet available on the iPad.

iPad office suites

The iPad is more than an Internet-enabled gaming slate. With the addition of an office suite it can replace your regular Mac or PC for light business tasks, using either the on-screen keyboard or a third-party add on. Here are four of the best.

If you only ever use your iPad to check your e-mail or browse the web when you're away from your computer you're only using half of its features. With a bright, generous 9.7in screen, it's also a first-class, lightweight business tool. Once you get used to the idea of typing on its glass surface it's almost good enough to tempt you to leave your MacBook or notebook PC at home.

Even if you don't get on with the on-screen keyboard, Apple's Bluetooth keyboard and alternatives provided by a handful of third-party manufacturers let you type away in comfort without ever touching your screen.

This opens up a whole world of office suites, which allows you to stay productive on the move while travelling with nothing more than your iPad. With Microsoft's Office formats now widely used, to the point where they can be considered an industry-standard, and with online services such as Dropbox, Google Docs and SugarSync making it easy to share data across multiple devices, the iPad really can be the hub of your mobile office.

Over these 11 pages, we have tested four of the best-specified iPad office suites, including Apple's own iWork, to see how well they stand up in a business environment. What is it like to create and edit documents using these tools, how easy is it to get your data off the iPad without syncing your device to iTunes? In short, which is the best choice for day-to-day use?

My Documents
12:49
Project Proposal
COMPANY NAME
228 words
macally

Documents To Go Premium

£9.99 from *http://bit.ly/giEeBj*

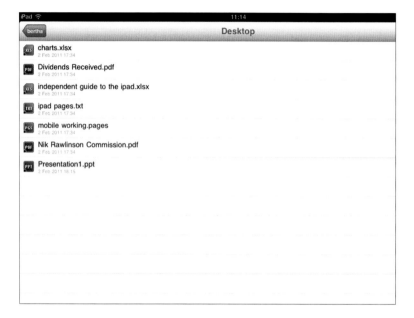

Documents to go has long been the go to application for working on the move. Its heritage stretches back to the earliest PDAs, but the iPad's larger screen really lets it fly.

It can open and create Microsoft Word, Excel and PowerPoint files, and view PDFs and iWork documents. It works just as happily with files on Google Docs, Box, Dropbox, MobileMe or SugarSync as it does with those on your desktop or laptop computer. A companion application for Mac OS X and Windows lets you pair your iPad with your computer and synchronise files wirelessly. It is by far the best implementation for file sharing we have seen among the products on test here.

The file management interface could do with a little polish. It works perfectly, but doesn't have the visual appeal of Quickoffice. Neither does the word processor, which presents you with a plain, blank typing area. This may well reduce distractions, but we much prefer Quickoffice or Pages' editing environments.

Formatting tools appear at the bottom of the screen and cater for a wide range of layout requirements including, impressively, multilevel numbered lists, superscript and subscript, strike through and double strike through and even hanging lines. Line spacing needn't just be single, double or line and a half, but multiples, point

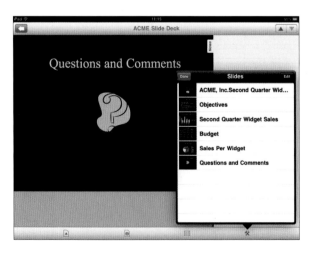

measurements, or minimum requirements, depending on your layout needs.

The word count panel tots up words, characters, characters with spaces and paragraphs. There are five fonts to choose from, including Calibri and Cambria, which are found in the latest editions of Microsoft Office on the PC and Mac.

The spreadsheet has a neat way of handling multi-sheet documents. A button to the right of the input bar flips the active view around on itself to reveal the spreadsheet's various pages. These can then be swiped until you find the one you need, at which point an upwards swipe swivels back to your document. It's simple and very effective.

Cells can be formatted as regular text, number, currency, date or time, with the various options taking their defaults from your iPad's geographical settings. Functions are invoked by tapping a button to the left of the input box, which calls down a categorised list with each one accompanied by an explanation of its variables, although no hints as to what it does, like you get in Quickoffice.

Resizing rows and columns is a simple matter of dragging their dividers in the margins, and tapping

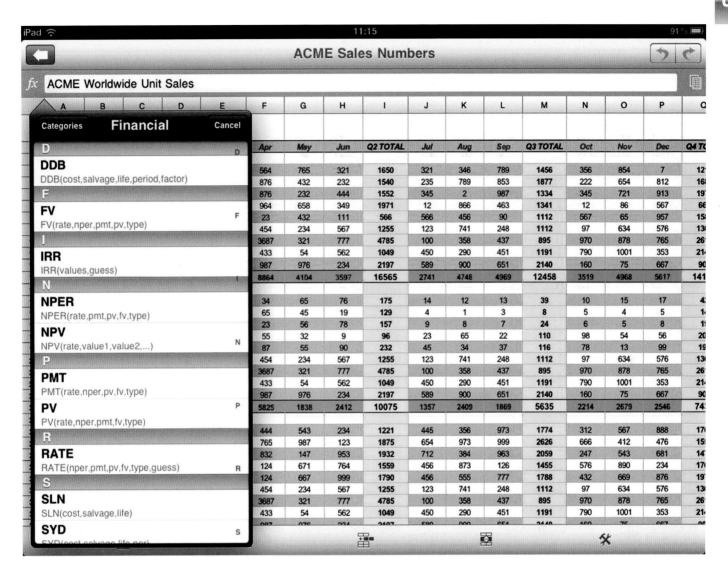

the freeze panes button will freeze everything above and to the left of your currently selected cell so that it remains static while the body of the sheet scrolls about the screen. Selecting multiple cells is easy – just double tap on the first cell of your range and then drag your finger across to the last; there's no need to worry about grab handles.

Sadly, the PowerPoint module is Documents to Go's weakest point. You can only edit PowerPoint documents if you have paid for the premium edition, and if you were planning to knock up a last-minute presentation while travelling to a meeting the results may make it obvious that you hadn't planned well in advance.

Text on a slide is all bullet- or list- based and must be added through the outline view, not directly to the graphical slide. The are no tools for adding images or shapes as there are in Keynote and

Quickoffice, and when working with a PowerPoint document created on your Mac or PC, while it correctly imports any embedded images, it doesn't make them available for editing in Documents to Go, which reduces the degree to which you can make serious last-minute changes.

When playing back your presentation, you may wish to take advantage of the opportunity to switch to full screen, but while this loses the toolbar – as you would want – it also loses the navigation buttons, and doesn't get rid of the notes tab that peaks in on the right-hand side of the screen.

Documents to Go certainly has plenty to recommend it – in particular the simple wireless synchronisation that doesn't require any online accounts or a physical connection to your Mac – but both iWork and Quickoffice have more compelling reasons to buy.

iWork

£5.99 per application

Pages: *http://bit.ly/gBubvR* / Numbers: *http://bit.ly/fRaAmE* / Keynote: *http://bit.ly/ffXrw0*

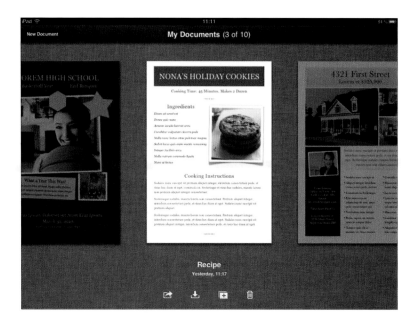

iWork comes in three parts, with the various components – Pages, Numbers and Keynote – bought as individual separate downloads. Each one costs £5.99. Selling it this way is a smart move on Apple's part for two reasons. First, it recognises that not everyone will need all three tools, and second it disguises the fact that buying them all is actually fairly expensive. With the App Store's pricing working as it does, many customers would have to think very carefully about spending the combined price of £17.99 on a single suite. Splitting it into three parts, at £5.99 a pop, softens the blow.

That said, what you get your money is certainly impressive. Pages, like the desktop version that runs on the Mac, is as much a basic layout tool as it is a word processor. This much is evident from the 16 impressive templates that act as a starting point to all your work. One of these is blank for regular writing, but the others are classic and formal letters, posters, recipes, flyers and so on.

Once you've chosen one, you can tweak it to meet your particular needs, and those tweaks really are impressive. Drop a star on the page, for example, and you can simply drag to change the number of points or the sharpness of each one. Do the same with a polygon, and you can drag in just the same way to change the number of sides down as far as three or up as far as 11. Each shape is contained within a bounding box with grab handles on the sides and corners. Dragging these changes the shape's proportions, and when parts of it lineup, such as the corners at 45 degrees or the centre or edges with other elements on the page, dynamic guidelines appear as they do in full-blown layout tools like InDesign CS5, to keep you on track.

It can handle headers and footers, and you get a proper view of your page layout, complete with margins. These are set by dragging them in a document setup screen, which also displays the paper's physical dimensions. There is a full-screen view for distraction-free working, as there is in

iWriter, and in recent editions this works in both landscape and portrait orientation.

The interface is nothing short of beautiful, with a touch of retro to it, and there's a smart button on the toolbar that lets you break pages or columns, insert a line break or tab. There's a massive 56 fonts to choose from, including Zapfino, Gill Sans and Futura, but to save you from creating a mess on the page, this is a style-based word processor. Once those fonts have been assigned to styles, you can pick them from the toolbar to ensure consistency throughout your document. Pages is a joy to use and well worth the money.

Numbers is equally good-looking. It, too, is a template driven application, giving you plenty of jumping off points from which to start working. It will let you import Excel documents and, like Pages, can work with files hosted on MobileMe or a WebDAV server.

Its key selling point is perhaps the four customised keyboards that help enormously when entering complex data, such as dates and formulae, and are selected automatically depending on the format of the cell in question.

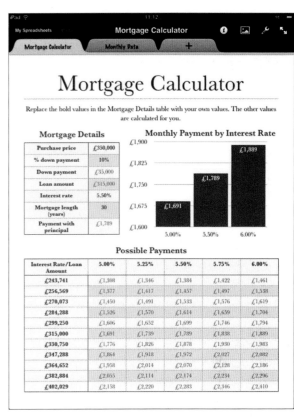

Keynote is the must-buy application for anyone who regularly presents on the move and doesn't want to travel with a Mac. Even if you never create any slideshows on the iPad itself, its ability to import Keynote files from your Mac – and PowerPoint presentations – means you can travel with little more than a portable screen and still make a good impression. The ability to tweak your presentation at the last minute before delivering it to your audience is of course an added bonus.

Like Pages and Numbers, Keynote features a broad selection of templates from which to work, and its image manipulation tools, like those in Pages, have plenty of visual hints that help you maintain the proper dimensions in every instance. Images can be resized within their bounding boxes, swapped out or removed altogether. Slide transitions are fully adjustable so that they can run faster or slower depending on your requirements, and on-slide elements can build individually.

The various iWork applications can print to AirPrint compatible printers, but they aren't as versatile as Office2 or Quickoffice when it comes to sharing files or working with remote documents. Naturally, Apple is keen to push MobileMe and iWork alongside e-mail as the primary medium for sharing, and so support for third-party services such as Dropbox and Google Docs are notable by their absence.

We reiterate that buying all three components of iWork is expensive, but if you only need one then £5.99 is a fair price to pay for an application that's both beautiful and a joy to use.

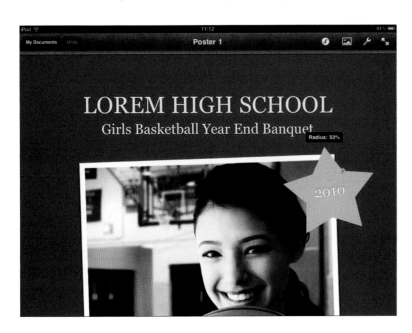

Office2 HD

£4.99 from *http://bit.ly/gll9NS*

Office2 is a word processor and spreadsheet combo for both the iPad and the iPhone. It uses each device's internal storage for local work, but can just as easily work with files stored on MobileMe, Google Docs, Dropbox, mydisk, Box, iCloud or your own WebDAV server. This means you can work on the same documents at the office and on the go without having to think about transferring them from one device to another. It also means that if you work with files directly on the server you don't need to worry about misplacing your iPad and losing your work.

It's not a particularly attractive suite and doesn't have the style of either iWork or Quickoffice. However, it is well featured. Word compatibility includes .docx files, although Excel support stretches only to version 2003 (.xls).

The word processor handles all regular formatting options such as bold, italic, underline, fonts of various sizes and faces, and colour. Images can easily be inserted into documents using the media drop-down, which works much like the media browser on a Mac, and it has 24 table presets in four different colours. There's even an option to print straight from the application if you have a compatible printer.

There are eight fonts to choose from, including Arial, Courier New, Helvetica and Times New Roman in sizes running from eight point to 72 point. The interface is minimal, with just a single row of tools running across the top of your document and your folders and files in a panel to the left. This panel can be collapsed, and it disappears on its own when you turn the iPad to portrait orientation, but in neither instance does Office2 give you an accurate view of the page itself, complete with margins and edges.

A brief stats panel counts words, characters with and without spaces, and paragraphs, making it suitable for students or anyone else who must write reports and assignments to a fixed length. There's a

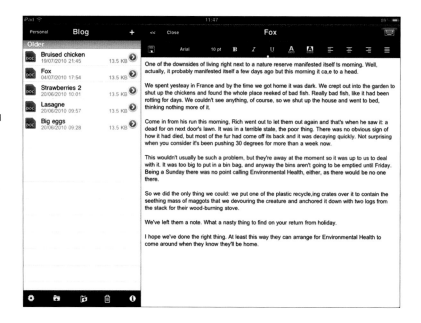

built-in spell checker that underlines mistyped words that haven't been auto corrected by the iPad itself, but no option to perform a document wide spelling check manually.

We were very impressed by the colour selection tools, which are present in both the word processing and spreadsheet modules. When you first tap the colour button you're given a choice of 16 additive, subtractive and mixed colours, but tapping the More Colours button lets you mix your own by dragging a hue slider, which opens up an impressive 648 different tones. The slider is slightly off centre, so doesn't quite match up with your finger as you drag, but once you know this it's easy enough to work with.

The spreadsheet doesn't feature Numbers' helpful multiple keyboards, but a function button on the toolbar gives you quick access to a lot of advanced terms, each of which is linked to a brief help panel that tells you what the function does and how to use it if you've selected it in an inappropriate position.

Spreadsheets are quick and easy to format. Column widths and row heights can be adjusted by

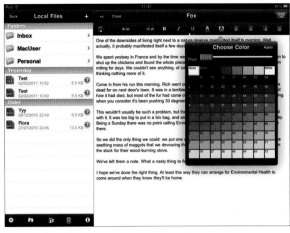

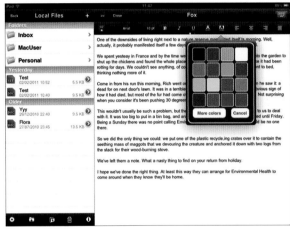

dragging their borders or a slider in a dedicated panel. There's even text wrapping within cells for particularly long strings of text. Cells can be given borders, although they're all of the same width, and all in black, but when combined, these basic formatting features will let you knock up some good looking spreadsheets that could be used without needing any additional polish when you get back to the office.

There are four currency options – dollar, pounds sterling, euro and yen – and rudimentary sorting options, organising data horizontally or vertically, by column, and in ascending or descending order. You can't sort along rows.

Columns and rows can be frozen so that they remain in view while the rest of the sheet scrolls around. This is handled in a particularly neat manner. If you're in column A, tapping the freeze button will hold all of the rows above it. If you're in row 1, it will freeze all of the columns to its left. If you're anywhere else, all of the rows above and all of the columns to the left of the active cell will be frozen at once.

Cell selection in general is handled very well, with the blue spots that have become familiar from selecting text in Mail and other text-based applications appearing on the corners of cells if you rest your finger on them for long enough. They appear top and bottom, and dragging either spot out from the cell will select other cells in that direction.

Office2 HD may lack a presentation tool, but if your work revolves around writing prose and crunching numbers there's plenty to recommend it. It's plain but functional, and does what it claims very well indeed.

Quickoffice Connect Mobile Suite for iPad

£14.99 from *http://bit.ly/f3xdcN*

Quickoffice seems to offer the best of both worlds. It boasts the versatility of Office2, with the ability to work on documents hosted on MobileMe, Huddle, SugarSync, Dropbox, Google Docs and Box, alongside those stored locally on your iPad. It also has three integrated tools: a word processor, a spreadsheet and presentation program.

The file handling interface is both colourful and beautiful, and the document editing screens are simple and elegant. Quickoffice feels less 'designed' than iWork, but that is in no way a bad thing.

Although it doesn't use Microsoft's Office application names, it's clear what it's talking about when it gives you options to create presentations, spreadsheets and documents in 2003 and 2007 formats (2003-only for presentations), so you can handle the .xlsx and .docx Excel and Word formats. On top of this it can read and display PowerPoint 2007 files, but neither create nor edit them.

There aren't a great deal of formatting options in the word processor, but how many do you really need when you're writing on the move? It's sports seven fonts ranging from 8 to 72 point in size with bold, italic and underline for emphasis. It has basic outlining tools thanks to auto indentation, bullets for lists and a very smart way of setting alignment, in which you drag example text left and right in the paragraph formatting panel for left, centre and right justification. There is no full justification, no multi-column layout and no table tools for more complex writing jobs.

We do, however, love the writing environment. It's close to distraction free, with only the simplest of menu bar visible at the top of the screen, and when you hold your finger on the right of the screen, thumbnails of the pages in your document fade into view. Dragging your finger up and down scrolls them so that when you let go the largest thumbnail becomes the active page. It's an elegant, discreet solution that Pages and Office2 would do well to emulate.

Tap any cell in the spreadsheets and it's given four handles which, when dragged, select other cells adjacent to it. The drop-down menu handles adding and removing rows and columns and you can easily add borders to each one, although as with Office2, they are all the same size. A neat noughts and crosses style board lets you drag sample text within an alignment dialogue to any one of nine positions to horizontally or vertically align it within each cell. The same range of fonts and sizes is available here as in the word processor, and where the word processor let you set a highlight colour, the spreadsheets lets you pick cell colours.

Cell formats can be set to one of nine different types including accounting and scientific, and there are five currency options, encompassing dollars, pounds Sterling, euro, yen and CNY.

Again, the interface is charmingly unfussy and elegant, and switching between the sheets within your document is like turning the pages, complete with iBooks-like animation.

Formulae are well handled: tap the cell where you want to display the answer, and then the 'fx' button beside the input bar to call up a menu of available

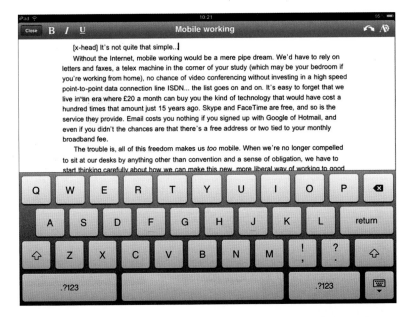

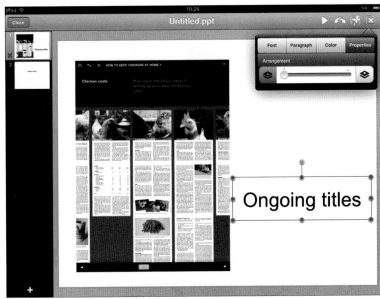

commands. Each one is accompanied by a hint bubble showing the expected formula format, and you can click on the cells containing the data on which you want to work to swap out the hint variables without worrying about the required operators. For example, choose 'sum' and then tap A1 followed by A2 and they will be dropped into the equation, along with the necessary '+' symbol.

The presentation module is very versatile, and the compact menu system centralises many key functions. Text boxes, for example, are added from the shapes menu. Shapes themselves can be resized and rotated, snapping every 45 degrees, although there are no guidelines to show when you're aligned with other elements. Neither is it

possible to change attributes of the shape itself, such as the numbers of points on a star or sides on a polygon simply by dragging as you can in iWork. You can, however, change their colours and rearrange the stacking order on your slides through the properties Inspector.

Like the spreadsheet, the presentation module presents a panel split into nine boxes to handle alignment within text boxes.

Quickoffice is certainly the most fully featured integrated suite on test. At £14.99 it undercuts iWork by enough of a margin to make it the most appealing offering here for anyone who will use all three components, and we'd argue that as you're paying just £3 more than you would for any two iWork components it's probably worth the extra just so you can edit all three document types 'just in case' if you were planning on buying more than one iWork app anyway.

For those who will use only one part, though, we'd recommend Pages, Keynote or Numbers, which at a penny shy of £6 for each one represent a saving worth making.

Editor's choice

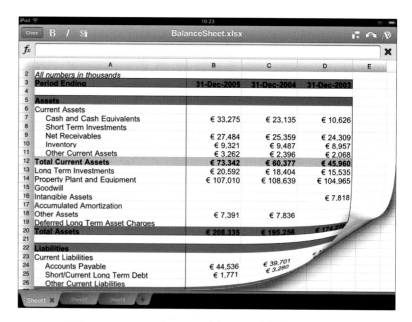

The four suites on test here each represent excellent value for money when compared to their desktop equivalents. If you got even half as many features on a regular Mac or PC for the same price you'd be more than happy.

The App Store pricing model, though, has led us to expect a lot for our money, so these suites have to work very hard to impress. By and large they did just that, and each had its own unique benefits.

Chief among them was Documents to Go's impressive wifi syncing. It really is an 'install and forget' feature that needs no maintenance and no complicated set-up beyond entering a four digit code to pair your two iPad and computer.

Sadly, though, Documents to Go was trumped by other suites on test here when it came to the actual office work in question. The writing environment was stark, and not nearly so inspiring as Quickoffice Writer or Pages. The spreadsheet earned it back a lot of ground, but the presentation tool fell short of Keynote and Quickoffice, which offered more extensive editing tools, allowing you to produce a more impressive presentation from scratch when out and about.

Office2 doesn't have a presentation tool, and again its word processor doesn't give you any hints as to how your work will look when printed. The spreadsheet lacks the helpful formula-building hints

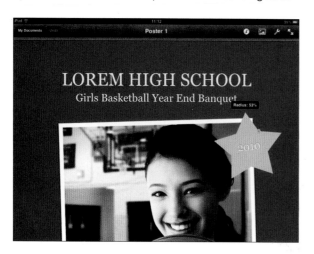

of Quickoffice and Documents to Go. It's a lovely suite that meets most needs, but doesn't offer a round enough package to come out top.

That leaves just iWork and Quickoffice. Both are well designed, but the various iWork tools have the edge. They are a pleasure to use, and neat features like the switchable keyboards in Numbers do much to enhance its appeal. The simple fact that Numbers implements two return keys, with one moving horizontally and the other vertically shows some smart thinking that recognises the way we work in a spreadsheet application.

Quickoffice is equally well designed, but in a more understated manner. Its bright colours, high quality icons and smart transitions, such as the page turns that move you through a spreadsheet, make it an appealing suite. Like Pages, its word processor gives you a clear idea of how your work sits on the page, and the presentation module can call on images in your iPad library to illustrate your work.

If you need to create more complex documents with advanced layouts then iWork's Pages is the best choice. If that's the case, and you also need a spreadsheet and presentation tool then we'd recommend sticking with Apple through and through and buying Keynote and Numbers, too.

However, for day to day office work we'd recommend you take a serious look at Quickoffice. Its less busy interface helps you focus more on your work than how it's formatted, it works out slightly cheaper than buying all three iWork applications, and its file handling is more flexible.

iPad applications

Our pick of the best downloads from the App store that will make your iPad more useful and fun every day...

080   BBC News

081   Dropbox

082   Epicurious

084   Evernote

085   Flipboard

086   IMDB

088   Penultimate

089   Reeder

090   Rightmove

091   SugarSync

092   TV Guide

093   Zinio

094   Evening Standard

094   France 24

095   The Guardian Eyewitness

095   Huffington Post

096   New York Times

096   Telegraph

097   ArtStudio for iPad

098   iFontMaker

098   Omnifocus for iPad

100   Pulse

101   Atomic iPad

102   Sonos Controller for iPad

103   eBay

104   Amazon Windowshop

105   Kindle

106   VNC Lite

107   TuneIn Radio

108   TED

BBC News

Free from *bit.ly/hwiYsu*

The BBC has just finished constructing its £1bn news centre in the heart of London, which can only be good news for those who rely on its services – among them the dedicated iOS apps for iPad, iPhone and iPod touch.

Initially available only to US iTunes Store customers, the BBC News app is now available in the UK, too. It's a free download, and works in both portrait and landscape orientation, in slightly different ways.

Hold it in portrait orientation and your attention is focussed on a tall reading pane, which is perfect for longer stories. Hold it horizontally, though, and the screen is split in two, with a wider selection of categories filling the left-hand side and the current story on the right. Swiping the categories shows you all the available headlines, each accompanied by a thumbnail image. Swipe the story pane left and right to move through the articles.

The BBC News app is effectively an impressive interface to the BBC's must-read news website, and it brings with it many of the site's most compelling features – in particular, excellent use of video.

The BBC's network of domestic and foreign correspondents is filing video content around the clock, much of which is embedded in the stories within this app. Tapping the videos opens up a YouTube-like player, which streams very efficiently on a domestic broadband connection, so you can keep in touch with the news wherever you happen to be in your home or office. There's also a button on the toolbar that takes you to live BBC output.

The app is customisable to the extent that it allows you to choose the categories that should be displayed in the left-hand pane and the size of the text used to render your stories, but that's it. Available categories include world and UK news, technology, sport, politics and health, among others.

With the growing importance of social media, it's no surprise to see that there are also tools for

sharing story content with your contacts on Facebook and Twitter, or by sending an email from within the app itself.

BBC News is by far our favourite current affairs application from any national broadcaster, with clear, concise, well-written stories told from a truly international standpoint.

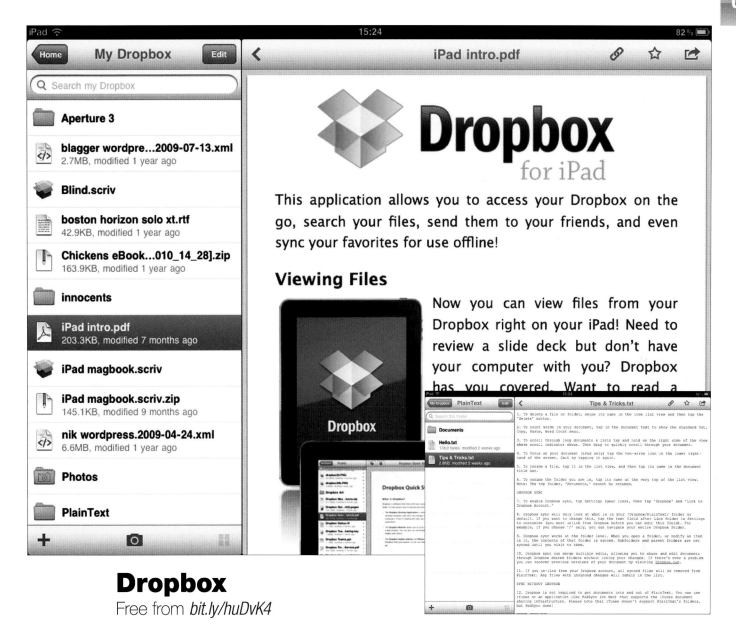

Dropbox

Free from *bit.ly/huDvK4*

Dropbox has long been one of our favourite tools for synchronising data between several PCs.

The idea is simple: set up Dropbox on as many machines as you want, and log in each to the same account. Whenever you drag a file into your Dropbox on one of those machines, it will be automatically synchronised with each of the others that share that account.

Now, with Dropbox available on the iPad, it takes on another role: it allows you to access those files wherever you happen to be, so long as you have a wifi or 3G connection.

Once logged in to your account, the iPad edition lets you manage your previously synchronised files,

deleting those you no longer need and emailing links to the ones you want to share with your colleagues.

You can create new folders and add images from your photo roll, but the real power of Dropbox starts to become clear when you pair your account with third-party tools, such as Quickoffice (see our Office Suites test) to use it as a remote cloud storage device for saving your work.

Using Dropbox in this way means that your files will immediately become visible in the Dropbox application itself, transforming this app in to a first-class file management tool, like Windows Explorer or Mac OS X's Finder. For all Dropbox members, this is a must-have download.

Epicurious

Free from *bit.ly/g0eAhh*

If all cookery books were as beautiful as Epicurious, we'd all be a whole lot better fed. This lush digital edition is so tempting, it's making cooking fun again.

Epicurious is a advertising-supported cooking encyclopedia, packed full of recipes, expertly sorted by a powerful search tool.

The front page changes over time with seasonal suggestions such as Christmas treats, Super Bowl snacks or Romantic Dinners for Valentines' Day. Opening any one of these categories shows you suitable food for the occasion in question.

Each recipe is rated by other users, with one to four forks denoting how well it has been received, so you know a four-fork review is going to be a winning meal. The instructions are clear and well-written, and although there is usually no more than one image per recipe, you don't need step-by-step shots to follow along.

The default font size is fairly large, but can be shrunk or enlarged, and there's a neat orange marker in the margin that you can drag up and down the recipe to keep your place.

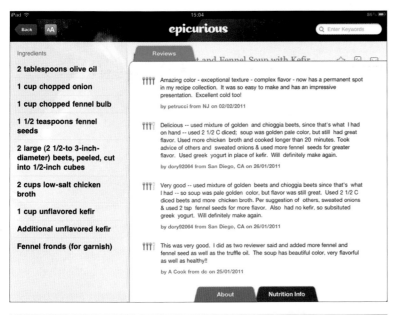

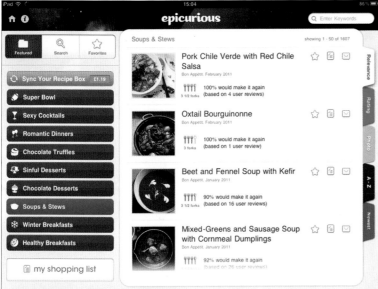

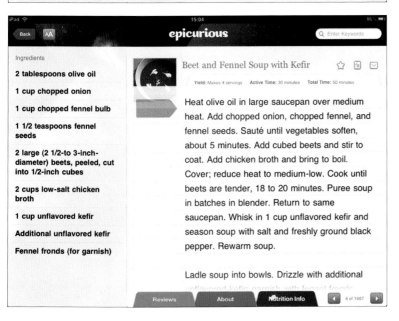

Epicurious has built up a strong community following, and beside the fork ratings there are short user reviews, which pop up when you tap on the Reviews tab at the bottom of each recipe. Often these are more than a simple verdict on the quality of the menu, but add helpful hints and changes to the ingredients list that other users have found work in their experience.

It should be noted that the recipes usually have a US bias, so users from other parts of the world may have to translate some measurements, from imperial to metric, or from cup measurements to whatever local equivalent you understand.

If you really don't know what to cook, you can rank by ratings or view a gallery of images to see what whets your appetite. Our favourite, though, is to see what we have in the fridge and then do an ingredient search, typing those foodstuffs into the keywords box to see what it throws up.

When you've found your chosen recipe, one tap adds all of its ingredients to a shopping list. Adding further recipes adds their ingredients, too, so that by the time you've finished drawing up your menu you have a combined shopping list, ready to take to the shops. The ingredients are helpfully split into categories, such as fresh produce, baking, pantry items and so on, which should help organise your trip around the supermarket aisles. Each one is also accompanied by a check box which, when tapped, greys it out so that you know you've added it to your basket already.

Although the app itself is free, if you want to synchronise your recipe box across several devices it involves a small in-app purchase. You might want to consider this if you have both the iPad and iPhone editions, with the iPad app used for following recipes in the kitchen and the iPhone version carried about in the supermarket as you buy your supplies.

Epicurious is quite simply one of those special applications that lets the iPad really shine. So long as you're happy to use it in the kitchen and keep it out of the way of running taps or buttery fingers it is without question the future of cooking and baking. With more than 30,000 recipes to call on, it's also an app we can see ourselves using for years to come. If you want an idea of what Epicurious has to offer before installing it, though, check out the recipes online at *epicurious.com*.

Evernote
Free from *bit.ly/fsC3vS*

The iPad already has a note-taking application, so you might wonder why you want another one. The answer is: 'flexibility'.

Evernote isn't a purely iPad-only application, and while the iPad's native Notes app will only synchronise with Mail on the computer to which you sync it through iTunes, Evernote syncs wirelessly over the Internet to an unlimited number of other computers.

It works in a similar way to Dropbox: install the client application on as many PCs, Macs, iPad and iPhones as you like and sign in each one to the same account. Whenever you add a note to one installation it will then be synchronised with all of the others, with the tags, titles and categories in which it's filed copied across at the same time.

The Evernote client is free on every platform, and comes bundled with a generous bandwidth quota. This stretches to an unlimited number of notes and up to 60MB of transfers per month. No note can be larger than 25MB on the free account, but if you upgrade to a premium account at $5 a month or $45 a year you can add a wider range of note types, transfer 1GB a month and create notes of up to 50MB in size.

It's important to understand that a 'note' isn't only a plain text file, but could be a PDF file, an image or an audio file.

Evernote is supported by a broad range of third-party providers. Various Canon and Fujitsu scanners can scan direct to an Evernote account, Livescribe pens can port your handwriting and drawings, and Wacom Bamboo Pen Tablet users can create digital ink notes that synchronise to the service.

The benefit of the service only becomes evident when you use it on a daily basis, at which point it quickly becomes indispensable. The security of having all of your notes backed up on every Mac or PC you own, and on Evernote's servers, is certainly reassuring, too.

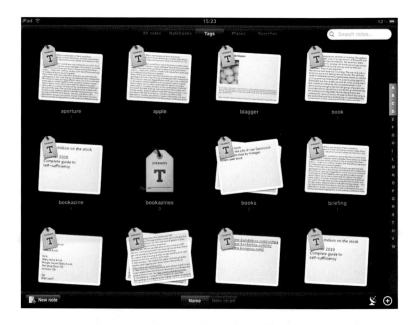

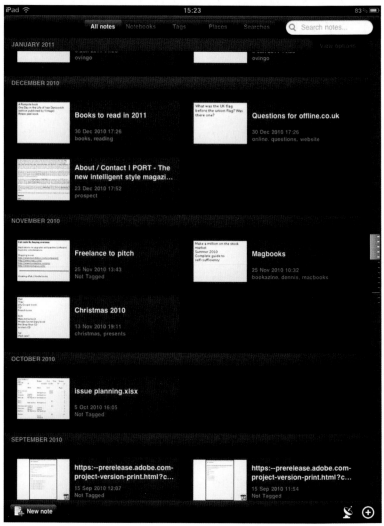

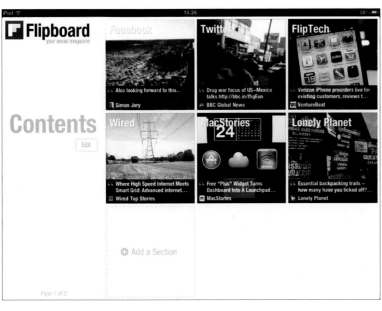

Flipboard
Free from *bit.ly/epgWuQ*

There's a whole host of Twitter and Facebook tools on the App Store, but this is one of the best-looking. Rather than presenting incoming Tweets and Facebook postings as a stream of raw text, it presents them in an attractive paned environment, pulling in referenced images and links to build up what can best be described as a social newspaper. Even the home screen is called a Contents page.

The Contents page consists of tiles, each one of which can link to a section, which might be your Flickr photos, Google Reader or a blog you enjoy reading online.

Open the Facebook section and you can not only read your friends' postings, but post comments and 'like' their contributions. The Twitter section lets you reply to Tweets, and it even threads related Tweets into a conversation.

Many online publishers are getting wise to Flipboard's increasing popularity and producing tailored content for the platform. These include the Oprah Winfrey Magazine, Wired Magazine and even MC Hammer. You may not have heard much from him since the 90s but, in the words of Rolling Stone magazine, he's a self-described 'super geek who's presently consulting for or investing in eight technology companies'. It's no wonder, then, that he chose Flipboard as the medium through which to debut his new track, 'See Her Face'.

As an increasing number of other publishers follow these trailblazers' leads, Flipboard looks set to become many users' first port of call when it comes to catching up with friends and celebrities thoughts in a more casual, engaging manner than the traditional social networks' websites, or largely text-based aggregators.

Apple named Flipboard, which was conceived when the developers tried to imagine what the web would look like if it was designed today from scratch, its iPad App of the Year in 2010. Time declared it one of the top 50 innovations of the same year.

IMDB

Free from *bit.ly/fausrK*

How often have you been sitting at home, watching television, and wondered where you've seen an actor before? If you're anything like us, it will be often. The Internet Movie Database (IMDB) has long been the turn-to site for all things cinema and TV, and for answering just this sort of question.

The only trouble is, unless you watch TV on your computer, you're willing to sit with a notebook on your lap or you can pause what you're viewing and shoot out to check something on your computer, it's not always convenient relying on an online source.

Fortunately, with IMDB on the iPad and iPhone it's now much easier to answer those niggling questions that can stop you concentrating on the rest of your film or programme.

Like all the best reference works, IMDB lets you keep on exploring and learning simply by tapping on the screen. Start by typing in the name of the programme or film you're watching and it'll throw up a list of possible matches, even if you've not got the name spot on. Pick the one you're after, and let the exploring begin.

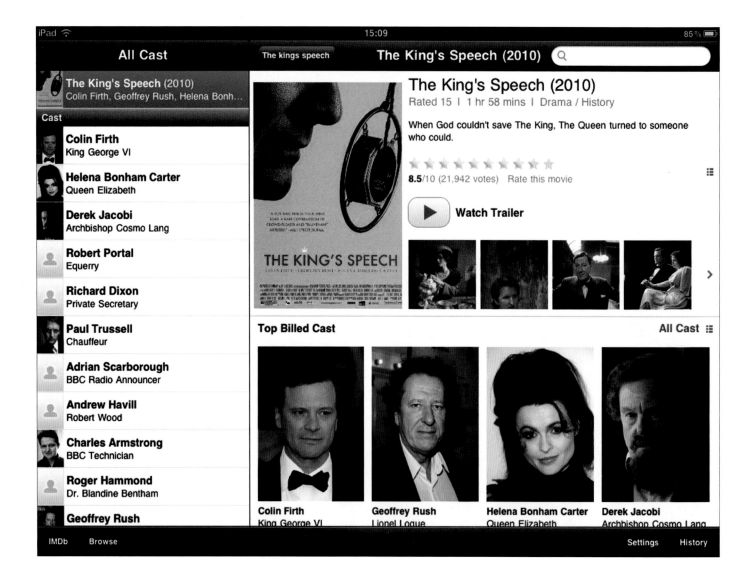

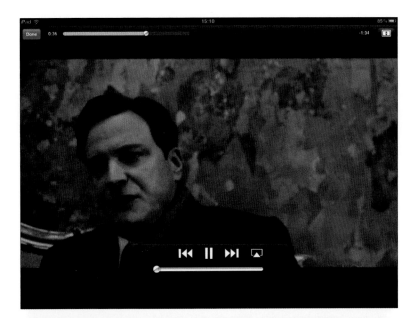

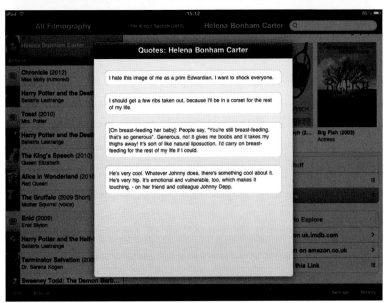

For starters, there's a synopsis of the programme in question, alongside a reader-voted rating. Often there's a link to a trailer – particularly if you've searched for a film – which can also be helpful if you're using the app to decide whether to head out to the cinema, rent or buy a movie.

There's also a full cast list, with impressively detailed run-downs of everyone featured. Tapping on any name take you to that artist's profile page, where you can see a full list of everything they have appeared in which, when clicked, takes you back to the start of the loop, with trailers, reviews and further cast lists. We would defy anyone to stop at just one click in this entertaining, addictive app.

Besides each character's filmography, there are short biographies, photo galleries and trivia facts with which to amaze (or bore) your viewing companions, depending on their point of view.

Recognising the fact that the various movie studios and TV broadcasters have got themselves a fairly strong grip on territorial control, the app lets you set a home reference site so that the material thrown up is relevant to your viewing location. There are seven to choose from, with the US, Germany, Spain, France, Italy and Portugal lining up alongside the UK.

Combine these broad geographical distinctions with your postcode and you can use the app to check what's on at cinemas close to your home. It draws up a list of what's new out this week, along with show times for each film in your local neighbourhood. If you only ever bought your local paper to check the cinema listings, this could well be enough to lose it a weekly subscriber.

When you've found a film you like, and you know it's on close to home, tapping on its entry in the listings gives you access to a whole host of professional reviews, which display on their publishers' websites within the IMDB window.

IMDB is a thoroughly exhaustive resource and is one of the few apps that we would recommend keeping close at hand the whole time you're watching a film or TV show. Clicking through its listings will give you a far better understanding of the network of actors, movies and programmes that underpin the industry, and help you discover new and classic material featuring your favourite actors that you may so far be missing.

Penultimate
59p from *bit.ly/gnt67l*

A lot of commentators were surprised when the iPad came out that such a large, glossy screen would be controlled not by a stylus but your finger. As we now know, of course, they needn't have worried: it works perfectly well, as demonstrated by Penultimate, where the 'pen' is your finger.

Penultimate transforms your iPad into a fully-featured sketchbook – or series of sketchbooks – in which you can draw quick illustrations or maps, or scrawl notes to yourself in handwriting.

There are three pens of various thicknesses to choose from, and six inks: black, two shades of grey, blue, green and red. Together they should be enough to help you distinguish between different parts of your notebook.

There are also three types of paper: graph, lined or plain, with whichever you select running through every page in your current notebook. The books

themselves can be renamed by tapping their titles in the organiser and their contents exported either by sending them as an email, or by synchronising them through iTunes.

As a means of recording brief ideas – particularly those that don't work well as typed documents in the Notes app – Penultimate is a quirky, useful and very popular tool, as evidenced by its performance in Apple's sales charts.

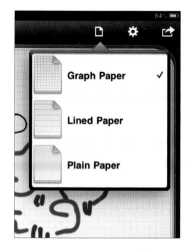

Reeder

£2.99 from *bit.ly/afbls5*

For browsing a large collection of RSS feeds, you won't find much better than Reeder. It makes excellent use of gestures for swift navigations and allows feeds to be organised in a hierarchy. Groups of feeds are shown as stacks of paper that display a name and the number of unread items that each one contains. The clever part is how you browse these stacks.

Tapping one shows headlines for the items from all of the feeds in that pile. However, placing two fingers on a stack and spreading them apart reveals the individual feeds in a neat grid. Tap one and you can read items from that source alone. The beauty is that the effect of each gesture intuitively makes sense.

A toolbar down the left of the screen contains buttons for switching between starred and unread items, and buttons to skip between stories. Selected settings are highlighted. Reeder packs in a couple of intuitive gestures with left and right swipes to toggle an item's read and starred status, and there are buttons that do the same at the top of the screen. Alongside them, you can share a story via Facebook, Twitter, Delicious, Instapaper, and Google Mobilizer, and copy and email links and articles.

Reeder syncs with Google Reader, though we suspect that, like us, you'll find it so pleasant to use that you'll begin to check the news on your iPad more often than your Mac or PC – particularly as it downloads each feed's content, which can then be read offline.

The only disappointment is the drab top-level navigation. The stacks of feeds could do with graphics to distinguish one from another. We would suggest a grid of site icons, much like iOS 4's folder icons. Keyword searches would also be a big improvement, but for straight browsing of feeds, Reeder's intuitive interface will win your heart.

If you want to keep on top of your Google Reader subscriptions, this is currently our top choice on the iPad, with its companion products on the iPhone scaling well to the smaller screen.

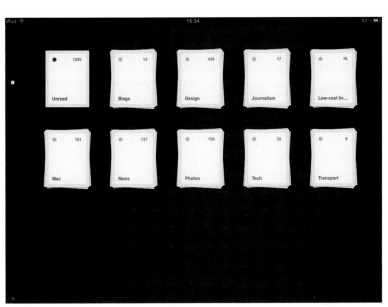

Rightmove

Free from bit.ly/ggj70c

Let's face it: we're all obsessed with houses and flats. Whether we're looking for our first purchase or somewhere new to rent, or we're checking on the value of our bricks and mortar investment, we all like to know whether the market's up or down, and what the insides of our neighbours' houses look like without arranging a viewing.

You can do both with this app, which lists property from the vast majority of British estate agents. If a house is for sale anywhere in the country, there's very little chance it *won't* be listed here, alongside a full description, a map and a gallery of interior shots, which are just perfect for the new generation of digital curtain twitchers.

Its powerful search tools greatly ease the task of researching your purchase, giving you scope to specify the number of bedrooms you need, what kind of property you're looking for, how close it must be to your chosen postcode or town and, perhaps most importantly, how much you can afford to pay. Helpfully this budget element includes not only a maximum price, but also a minimum.

Searches can be saved for future reference and individual properties can be set as favourites by tapping the star icon that sits on their top right corner, so you can build up a list of possibilities right away. Once you have your chosen few, an in-app form lets you email the agent directly.

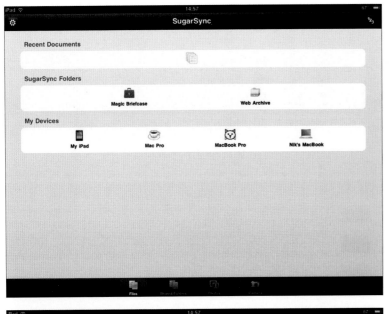

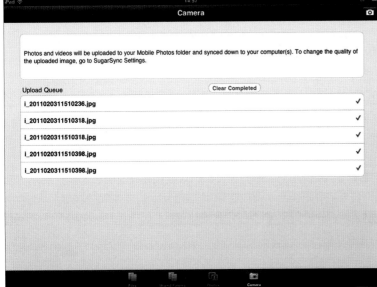

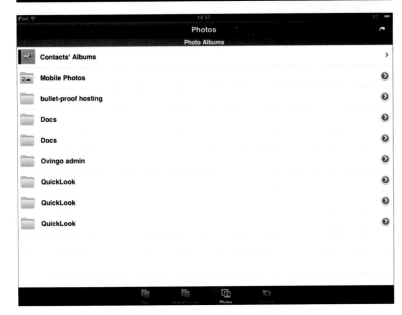

SugarSync
Free from *bit.ly/hb4ecC*

We have already discussed Dropbox and Evernote, two synchronisation tools that copy files between Macs, PCs and your iPad, so why would we want to cover SugarSync, which does something very much the same?

Several reasons. For starters, the way it works on your regular desktop machine is very flexible. Rather than having to file your documents and other data in the folders that *it* specifies, you can set up folders wherever you like and specify that SugarSync should then synchronise them.

Like Dropbox and Evernote, it gives you a free quota, which should be enough for most users, but if you find yourself using it so often that you exceed it, you can pay for an upgrade. These start at $4.99 per month or $49.99 per year for a 30GB account (the regular free account lets you synchronise 5GB).

The iPad app's interface is a fairly bland grey, but ignore this and focus instead on its features. Not only can you use it to view and manage your synchronised files, but you can also use it as a means of transferring images from your photo library back to your Mac or PC without using the Dock and USB cable.

This is done by opening the Magic Briefcase, which is a dedicated space used to drop random files that you need to quickly share between your various machines. Opening this on the iPad and tapping the Camera button followed by the option to take images from your library lets you tap on the pictures in your roll. They'll be added to an upload queue and automatically transferred to a Mobile Photos folder on your desktop machine. You can choose whether they are compressed in the process to preserve bandwidth and save time, or left at their native setting.

SugarSync performs a simple function (albeit with technical underpinnings) very well, and we'd recommend installing it at least for this photo transfer ability, if nothing else. The it does much more on multiple platforms increases its value.

TV Guide

Free from *bit.ly/eySoRe*

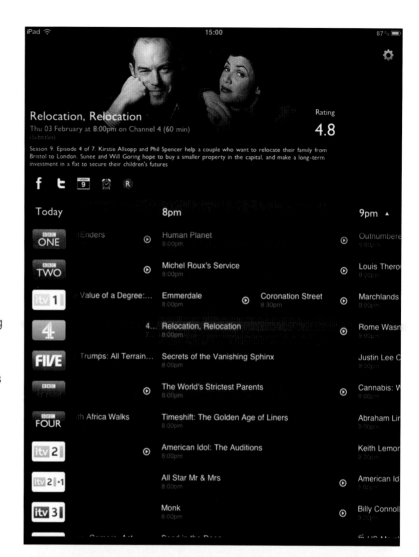

Unless you're an absolute TV addict, the chances are that you'll only buy a programme guide once or twice a year – at Christmas and Easter. The rest of the time, like us, you'll make do with the listings printed in the paper, on your digibox electronic programme guide, or online.

That's when TV Guide might well come in handy. This colourful app downloads the latest listings and displays them as a grid. A subtle vertical line running down through the grid shows you the current time, so you can see what is on right now.

Tapping a programme calls up a description of its contents at the top of the screen, and lets you perform a number of actions. Chief among these is Tweeting about the programme or posting it to Facebook, but you can also set a reminder about upcoming programmes. This will pop up five minutes before the programme is due to start.

For more advanced planning, you can also add programmes to your iPad's calendar application, making a note of it in whichever calendar you prefer to make sure that it doesn't clash with any existing appointments.

Sky+ subscribers can go one step further and schedule a recording from within the app itself. Tapping the red circle with an R inside it, just below the programme description, will program your box to save it to its hard drive, ready for you to watch at a more convenient time.

Several channels don't broadcast nationally, some have regional variations – such as the different BBC regions for the west, east, north and so on – and not everyone will be subscribed to the same satellite or cable line-up. In these instances you'll want to tailor the range of channels that are shown on the grid on your iPad. Doing this is a simple matter of tapping the cog icon and picking 'Select Channels', where you can specify your system – Sky, TalkTalk, Freeview and so on – and the region in which you live, as well as specific channels from each system's selection.

Zinio magazine newsstand

Free from *bit.ly/huoN0I*

Save yourself the hassle of carrying around bulky magazines, and save the forests from destruction at the same time, by switching to digital publications. A whole host of domestic and foreign titles have chosen to supplement their regular printed journals with digital facsimiles, courtesy of Zinio.

This clever system consists of a reader with a built in store, which works in much the same way as the iTunes Store. You can browse titles and buy individual copies of those that interest you, and them read on your iPad or a regular computer.

You can also make significant savings by subscribing to digital editions of your favourite magazines in this way, in which case you won't need to remember to check the store for each new issue. When a new edition is available, you'll receive an email letting you know, and the next time you open the Zinio application, the cover of that issue will be displayed in your library, ready to be downloaded and read.

In many ways the experience is better than the paper equivalent, with web addresses linked to the relevant sites, and the ability to keep a whole back catalogue of issues on one handy device.

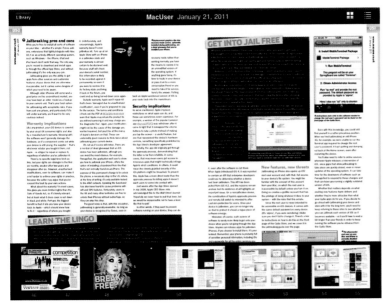

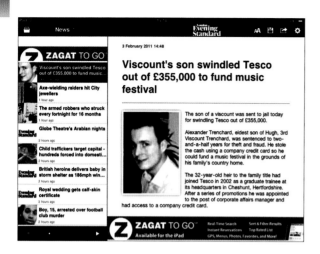

Evening Standard

Free from *bit.ly/gdgzgQ*

France 24

Free from *bit.ly/fBXrUl*

For many a London commuter, the Evening Standard is an essential read on their journey home. This long-standing tabloid paper was once a paid-for publication, but following a change of ownership it is now given away for free outside tube and train stations. It's also put in an appearance on the iPad.

We've certainly seen better-looking news applications, but that doesn't detract from the quality of the content. The Standard is updated throughout the day and its remit is incredibly broad. Those living outside of London will find plenty of interest, as it's certainly not an inward-looking provincial title.

Stories are organised into one of five different categories – news, business, sport, showbiz and life and style – with headlines displayed in a sidebar and the main part of the application given over to the associated story. There's some not-so-subtle advertising surrounding this, but as you're getting the content of a quality paper for free every day it's difficult to argue against this.

There are built-in sharing links for Twitter and Facebook, a link to open active stories in your browser, and an Email Article option that posts a link to the story – not the story itself – in a format that doesn't require the recipient to have an iPad to be able to follow the link.

There are so many reasons to download the France 24 application. If you're keen to improve your French language skills, then it's one of the best ways to get your hands on relevant, frequently updated French content. You're under no obligation to read the news in French, though, as you can switch to English and benefit from France 24's exceptional international journalism.

You can't help but notice the global focus of this app's content, which looks far beyond France's borders. Of the 19 stories on its home screen at the time of writing, one concerned France, one the EU, and the rest were drawn from around the world, with excellent coverage of the Middle East.

Tapping the map view opens up a plan of the globe, with red push pins like the ones used in the iPad's Maps application picking out the locations of breaking stories. Unpinching on the map zooms in so you can more clearly see the cities in which each story is set.

The app is packed with video, with a dedicated Shows tab giving you access to France 24 TV content, and a box on the home screen relaying live broadcasts from the station, allowing you to keep an eye on the world from the comfort of your sofa or desk without turning on the TV. France 24 is a worthy competitor – or indeed companion – to the BBC News application.

The Guardian Eyewitness

Free from *bit.ly/h7q2YN*

Huffington Post

Free from *bit.ly/iagKfx*

If a picture really does speak a thousand words then this app alone is a whole library. It features the 100 latest additions to The Guardian's photo library, and really takes advantage of the iPad's beautiful vibrant screen.

Curated by the paper's picture editors, they are the best of the best of thousands of images coming in to the paper every day. Each is accompanied by a small caption, but tapping the image itself hides both this and the toolbar so you can enjoy it without distractions. It's a great way to explore one story a day through a different medium.

Better yet, though, tapping a button on the caption spins it around to reveal a pro tip. These are short, and not always particularly in-depth, but they do give you a better understanding of how the image was shot. The tips are wide-ranging and varied, covering not only lighting and conditions, but also why the image composition makes each photo a success. For anyone who wants to work in photography or simply improve their shooting skills they really are invaluable pointers from those in the know that could help make you a better photographer.

Any image that particularly catches your eye can be saved as a favourite, and you can email or Tweet links to your favourites, or post them to Facebook to share with your friends.

Huffington Post is one of the most successful online-only newspapers in the world. Founded by Arianna Huffington and Kenny Lerer in 2005, it was snapped up by AOL in early 2011.

It has an excellent record of updating its reader application every few months, with the latest edition at the time of writing featuring an illustrated sliding interface that lets you scroll through the various stories in each section in a similar way to the BBC News application.

The Huffington Post has an extraordinarily loyal following, with posts often attracting several thousand comments. You can see why. The mix of long and short stories have the kind of gravity, depth and authority you would associate with a long-established broadsheet newspaper, which is truly impressive and goes to show how the Internet and tablet devices like the iPad have changed the news business.

The breadth of its content is amply demonstrated simply by scrolling through the category list, which includes not only the regulars – news, sport, health and so on – but also more esoteric choices, including 'Impact', Green and Divorce.

It is a US-based publication, with specific city content, but that doesn't mean it's entirely inward-looking. Its excellent international coverage makes it a first-class supplement to regular UK sources.

New York Times

Free from *bit.ly/edlN5X*

Telegraph

Free from *bit.ly/ha40b7*

Like the Telegraph (right), the New York Times application downloads stories from each day's edition, rather than the full newspaper, making them available offline.

The presentation is quite old fashioned, but this surprisingly works extremely well on the iPad's screen. Whether in portrait or landscape orientation the text-dominated index pages give it a weighty, authoritative feel, and we love the story pages themselves, which are split into columns. Reading them feels very much like reading a traditional printed newspaper.

When you download the app you get immediate access to four key sections from the paper – Top News, Most Emailed, Business Day and Video – and to access the rest you can either sign in with an existing paid-for New York Times account, or sign up within the application. When you do, you'll be able to read all of the paper's content from the full 25 sections within the application, including photos and video. Combined, they provide a balanced overview of world events.

This is just one of the New York Times' applications for the iPad and iPhone. The others are NYTimes Crosswords, NYTimes Real Estate and NYTimes The Scoop, which is a travel guide to New York, so of most use to anyone who lives there or is planning a trip to the city.

The Daily and Sunday Telegraph logically share an application, simply called 'Telegraph'.

Before we go any further, let's clear up one thing: this free application doesn't present the whole of each day's issue of the paper. If it did, it's unlikely any iPad owner would ever buy The Telegraph again. Instead it contains a 'best of' selection, which is downloaded every day when you start the app. This is a major benefit, as it means that once you have completed the download you don't need to be online to read it, so you can download it over breakfast and catch up with the news on your train ride to work.

The 'best of' runs to a very generous selection, covering domestic and world news, comment, features, sport and business. They're split into sections for easy navigation, and the simple interface is well thought out.

Swipe a story left or right to view the previous or next entry in the list, and tap the tab that protrudes from the left-hand side of the screen to call up a list of headlines with snippets for each story giving you an overview of the day's news and a way to skip straight to the story that interests you.

The presentation is very simple, giving over almost all of the screen to the story you're reading in a fairly large font. Some way of changing this font size would, though, be a welcome addition.

ArtStudio for iPad

£3.59 from *bit.ly/h9m78c*

Photoshop Express for the iPad is all about tweaking photos, so you'll have to look elsewhere to create something out of nothing. Step forward ArtStudio for iPad, which presents a clean slate on which to sketch out the ideas in your head.

Tapping a semi-transparent arrow reveals the toolbar, which provides access to swatches, layer controls and a toolbox full of essentials such as a pen, brush and a clone stamp that samples from one or all layers.

When appropriate, diameter and opacity sliders appear at the top of the screen. Less obvious to

begin with is that holding a tool's icon reveals a full palette of options. That also works to access blending modes, masks and a colour wheel on the main toolbar. Tapping with three fingers displays a shortcuts menu, with 100% zoom and fit to screen options.

Photos can be imported to turn into overpainted illustrations, or to apply filters. However, you can't finely adjust the intensity of blur and sharpen operations.

You might even use the app to brainstorm with colleagues, since it works with Apple's video output cables. Canvases can be up to 1024 x 1024 pixels, and they can be exported as layered PSDs for refinement.

Its toolbox is impressive in its scope, with 30 brushes, including a creative wet brush and the ability to create your own brushes up to 128 x 128 pixels in size. There are nine layer blending modes, layer masks, adjustments such as dodge and burn and a massive 44 fonts. It can even handle transparency.

Artistic novices needn't be put off by their lack of talent, as ArtStudio for iPad includes 17 drawing lessons, encompassing animals and humans, as well as how to handle perspective and 3D.

The inescapable limitation is that the iPad's screen is not sensitive to varying pressure levels. On top of that, painting with fingers is like Marmite, you'll either love it or hate it, though the offset painting mode stops your fingertip obscuring your handiwork. Regardless, ArtStudio is a great way to record your ideas whenever and wherever they occur.

Many reviews compare this to other iPad art apps, including Photoshop Mobile, and it more than holds its own.

If you don't believe us, check out the impressive gallery of images created in the app on Flickr at *flickr. com/groups/artstudioimages*

iFontmaker
£4.99 from *bit.ly/e8o98l*

Omni Focus for iPad
£23.99 from *bit.ly/eMOEFO*

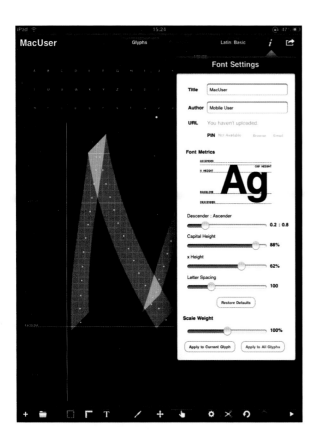

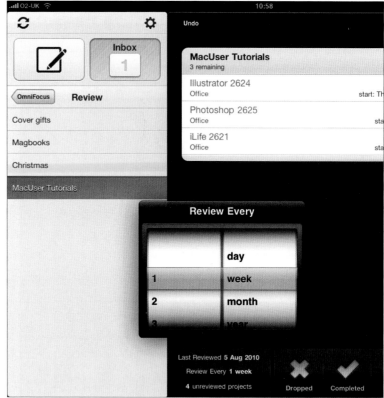

iFontMaker lets you construct TrueType fonts. Optional rulers mark up crucial font metrics for ascenders, cap height, x height, the baseline and descenders, all of which can be adjusted. You can adjust the default letter spacing, too. Switch to Compose mode and you can specify a string to see how well your letter forms work together.

You build them with pen and brush tools. The paint brush gives a smoothed stroke; the pencil has a rougher result. You can draw two-point lines too, or drag a calligraphy pen that leaves a trail of points. All tools let you adjust the stroke width, and you can move, scale and deform individual strokes by dragging the points from which they're formed.

However, there's no way to adjust these strokes by dragging handles. The deforming tool presents an obstacle when you demand absolute precision. Your creation is turned into a TrueType file by sending it to an online server.

OmniFocus subscribes to David Allen's Getting Things Done (GTD) method for managing your tasks in order to maintain your productivity. When you think of something that needs to be done, you tap a button to set up a new task. Those that fit in the remit of an existing project are easily assigned to it, while amorphous ideas that might later grow into their own projects can be saved to the inbox, where they'll wait until you can spend more time on them.

Tasks can be assigned a rough level of urgency: in the next few days, a week's time, or much further into the future. Setting exact deadlines isn't really part of the GTD method. Instead, OmniFocus is more about keeping on top of all the individual things that you need to do. Viewing that information in appropriate ways is crucial to maintaining your focus and your productivity.

OmniFocus has several ways to help you do that. First, you can view tasks by the projects to which

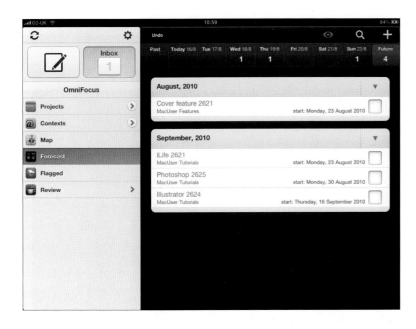

make appropriate preparations to ensure that you can complete every task that needs doing at a location. Location-based contexts can be created based on where you are, by browsing to them on a map or by entering an address. Contexts that happen to be locations can be plotted on a map with tags. Tap one and you'll see the relevant tasks. However, since contexts don't have to be based on locations, you can view them in the plainer style that's also used by the Project overview.

The forecast page shows the week ahead, with overdue projects clearly flagged in red, immediate tasks broken down by day of the week, and upcoming events highlighted so you can begin to focus your mind on them. Tasks flagged as important are collated in one location in the sidebar. Disappointingly, the Review section didn't display a numeric badge even when several of our projects were overdue an inspection, so you'll need to get into the habit of checking in.

The iPad's larger screen makes the app much easier to get to grips with than the iPhone version. In fact, you could even forgo the Mac version in favour of this one, which is less than half the price. With a MobileMe account, you don't even need the Mac version to sync data between your iPad and iPhone, as the apps can use iDisk, Omni's beta Sync Server, or another WebDAV server. You can't sync the iPad and iPhone apps directly, though. That also means you can back up the files created on the server to avoid losing everything.

The app works better in landscape orientation because the top-level navigation is always visible in the left pane. In portrait, this gets tucked behind a button in the toolbar, much like your folders do in Mail.

Despite this minor irritation, OmniFocus for iPad is worth the price tag to keep on top of your life. A few dummy tasks are already set up to help you take your first steps, and you'll soon find it a compelling way to keep on top of your workload.

they belong. Alternatively, you can look at contexts. They might sound like the same thing, but a context could be a location rather than an end goal. That's helpful if you work at different sites, perhaps freelancing for various companies or maintaining IT infrastructure for one that's spread over a large area. By assigning a context as well as a project, you can

Pulse
Free from *bit.ly/hdxPcl*

Pulse is a news reader that lets you browse RSS feeds visually. Instead of showing a textual list of news sources, feeds are shown as rows on screen, with each story afforded a small rectangular space. Swiping horizontally scrolls through a feed, and swiping vertically scrolls through your subscriptions.

You can personalise Pulse by tapping the cog at the top-left of the screen. The first settings tab allows you to reorder and delete sources, while the other three are for adding them: by specifying a URL, picking from the developer's recommended shortlist, or from your Google Reader account. Sensibly, this pane sticks around until you are finished and dismiss it.

Bear in mind that your feeds are stored in a flat list. There's no folder hierarchy, so it's best to keep the list fairly short. It works best with sources that use strong imagery to set items apart. For text-only feeds, you're better off with a traditional reader, but with the right sources, Pulse becomes an eye-catching way to consume news.

Tapping a story reveals a large pane with two tabs. One shows the plainer RSS summary of the story, while the other shows the article in its original web form, in case the summary isn't the full thing. If you're holding the iPad in portrait orientation, the feed's thumbnails run across the bottom of the screen, while in landscape you get a pane that shows two stories from your feeds down the left. Both remain interactive, and there's a button to get back to the full-screen index.

Stories can be shared via email, Twitter and Facebook, and stored in your Instapaper account. All popular choices, but it's not exactly a comprehensive selection of services. Heavy RSS users will find Pulse lacking, but if you're selective about the feeds you add to it, it's worth a look for its visual approach to browsing news, instead of purely reading headlines.

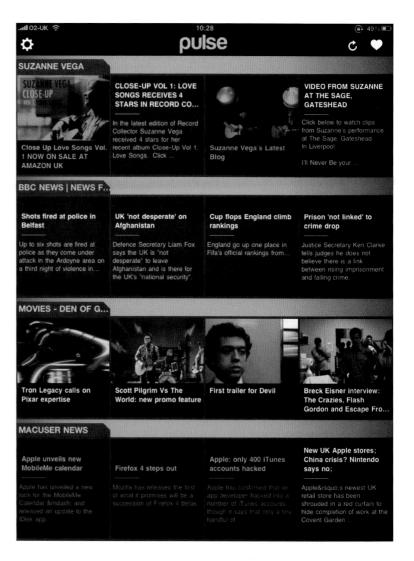

Atomic iPad

59p from *bit.ly/fXvwTw*

Browsing the web on Apple's touchscreen devices is so easy because of the gesture-driven navigation of pages. Atomic Web Browser develops that aspect, and it packs in some extra features that aren't found in Safari.

Its full-screen mode makes great use of limited screen space. You access it by tapping with three fingers, and you can place up to seven semi-transparent buttons over it to provide access to various features, which you get to pick.

Multiple open pages can be shown as traditional tabs or as a vertical list, complete with thumbnails. Both are faster to navigate than Safari's implementation. If you're only dealing with a handful of pages at once, you don't even need to use these mechanisms to get from one to the next. Just swipe left or right with two fingers.

That gesture, along with swiping up and down with two fingers and the three-fingered tap, can be overridden with a variety of other actions. These include going back and forward a page and jumping to the top of the page. Normally tapping the clock does that but you can turn it off to save even more space.

One of the great things about Atomic is that you can configure so many of its options to what works best for you. For instance, you can turn on just the status bar in full-screen mode to keep an eye on the time, while hiding the larger interface elements that consume a valuable portion of the viewing area.

There's also an ad blocker to which you can add your own domain filters, and you can stop images loading altogether. That's great if your network connection drops to GPRS or Edge speeds for a prolonged time.

The search bar works with several websites, including Google, Bing and Wikipedia, and more can be added. Sadly, the ability to search within the current page caused us problems when the item we were trying to find was in a Web 2.0-style collapsed section of the page.

The browser was also a bit less responsive in forms than Safari, even on our iPhone 3GS. Once a field had the focus it was fine, but the sticky pause beforehand is an uncomfortable throwback to when Apple's browser suffered from a similar issue.

Atomic is a universal app, so it makes full use of the iPad's increased screen resolution. And while full-screen mode isn't really necessary on that device, the additional gestures make browsing a bit more comfortable.

However, bookmarks aren't synced over MobileMe, so you can't keep them in sync with your Mac, although Atomic can import bookmarks exported manually. We'd also like to see integration with something like 1Password, especially as you can lock the browser with a Pin code, in case you leave your device unlocked.

Atomic wins out over Opera, which recently appeared on the App Store, as it retains the gestures you've learned in Safari and extends them. Even so, it's not perfect. If you tell it you want to see the same pages next time you open it, it reloads them all, putting an unnecessary load on the application. We hope this will change in an update, given that iPhone OS 4 allows apps to save their state when closed.

Sonos Controller for iPad

Free from *bit.ly/hQvekt*

The idea behind the Sonos Controller for iPad is that you've already spent hundreds of pounds on a versatile piece of kit, so you shouldn't need to buy a pricey £279 dedicated controller.

The software is styled a lot like the Mac application. The screen is split into several panes, from which you can select a zone (rooms that you've grouped so the same music streams to ZonePlayers in each one), find out what you're listening to, and choose a source. This can be an iTunes library that's been configured with the Mac OS X software, allowing you to queue tracks or create playlists for repeated listening. Searching works by scrolling or more directly by typing what

you're looking for. Alternatively, you can stream from a variety of online sources that Sonos supports, including free-to-listen Internet radio, last.fm and Spotify; the latter requires a paid subscription.

Last.fm integration is a joy, though, with the ability to listen to songs in your library or recommendations based on information it has collected about your listening habits. Sonos's kit sends this information to keep recommendations current. This is irrespective of whether your Mac is turned on. The app cuts it out of the equation and brings the Internet into the living room – or wherever your ZonePlayer lives.

The app significantly lowers the price barrier to this elegant music streaming kit.

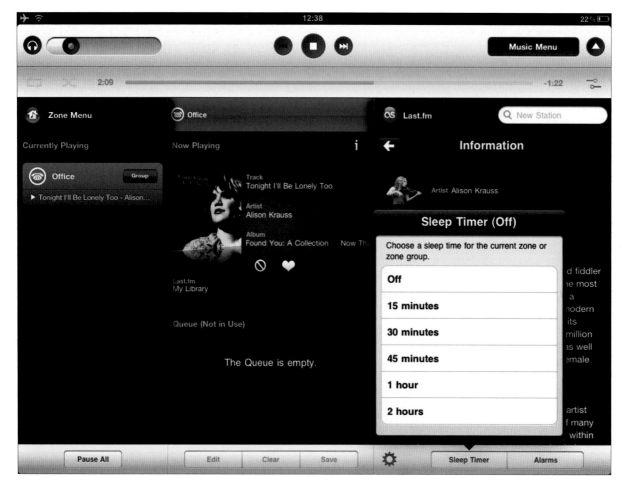

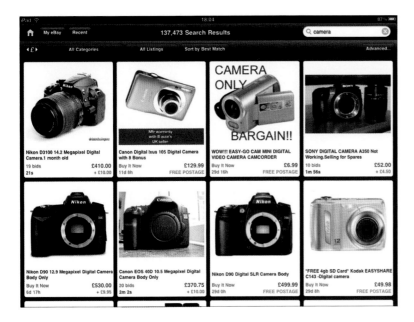

eBay
Free from *bit.ly/eNEouk*

It's surprising what a difference this application makes to the eBay shopping experience. eBay's site isn't exactly pretty, which is perhaps one reason for its success – it looks uncorporate and trustworthy – but this application significantly neatens things up. It lets you search for and browse listings on your iPad without having to fire up Safari, recreating the content of each listing, but significantly smartening up all of the clutter that surrounds them.

You start by typing an entry into the search box at the top of the screen. This brings up all matching results, which you can then go on to filter using the buttons above the picture tiles.

One button lets you focus on particular categories, another lets you choose listing types (auction, Buy It Now or store inventory), a third lets you sort on the regular eBay criteria (lowest price, distance and so on) and a fourth lets you filter by price. This is by far our favourite filter as its implementation is so simple and intuitive. Tap it, and rather than selecting from a drop-down list you're given a sliding bar at the bottom of the screen with price clusters marked on it by vertical blue lines. Dragging the left-hand edge of the bar towards the centre increases the specified minimum price; dragging the right-hand edge towards the centre reduces the maximum you are prepared to pay. When you let go, the bar resizes and the listings are updated to reflect your selection.

The app ties in to My eBay, so you can use it to monitor your watched items and inbox messages, as well as completing a transaction without ever touching your browser. It's the best, most convenient way to use eBay, by far.

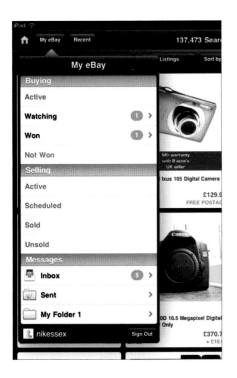

Amazon Windowshop
Free from *bit.ly/h393CT*

Amazon is the first place most of us turn when shopping for a whole host of products. It's no longer just a bookshop. With such an expansive inventory, though, navigating its online shop through the iPad's browser can sometimes be a chore. That's why Windowshop is such a boon.

Products are laid out in an attractive grid, with plenty of space given over to images. Search for the products you're after using the box at the top of the screen and then filter the results by category using the buttons on the toolbar below.

Tapping one of the image tiles flips it around and expands it to fill the screen to display the full details

for the product in question, with a tabbed display letting you switch between photos, details, reviews and related products. If you still want to spend your money, you can either add it to your basket or buy it immediately, and you can also see the new and used results if you want to make a saving.

Sadly it's not perfectly integrated with the Kindle Store (see right), so if you want to buy new books for your reader you are shunted out into a separate screen through which to peruse the catalogue and choose to which device you want your purchase delivered. Other than that, this is an attractive, engaging way to shop from your iPad.

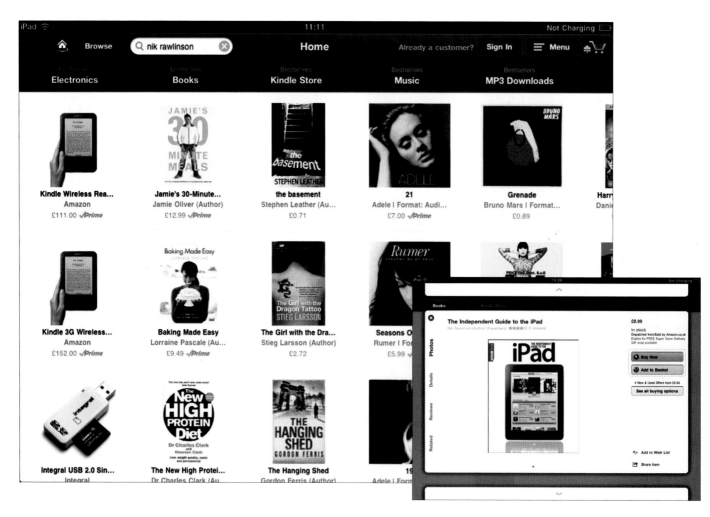

Kindle

Free from *bit.ly/dY9Ooo*

You may be wondering why we'd recommend downloading yet another electronic book reader when iBooks already enjoys such a powerful pull on the iPad. The answer is simple: choice.

If you could only ever shop in one high street bookstore you'd be forever wondering what is available elsewhere, and whether it's cheaper. Tied to Amazon's enormous online store, Kindle has access to more than half a million volumes, each of which can be downloaded and ready to read in less than 60 seconds.

Kindle runs on multiple platforms, including the iPad, iPhone, Mac, PC and, of course, the dedicated hardware Kindle electronic book device, so you can read your downloads using whichever device you have to hand. Whichever you choose, you'll always be reading from the same page, as Kindle's Whispersync technology automatically synchronises your current page on each device, along with all of your saved bookmarks.

The reading experience is pleasant, with six font sizes to choose from, the option of one or two columns per page, and white, black or sepia pages.

With Kindle and iBooks installed side by side on your iPad you'll have access to an unrivalled library whenever you feel the need to read.

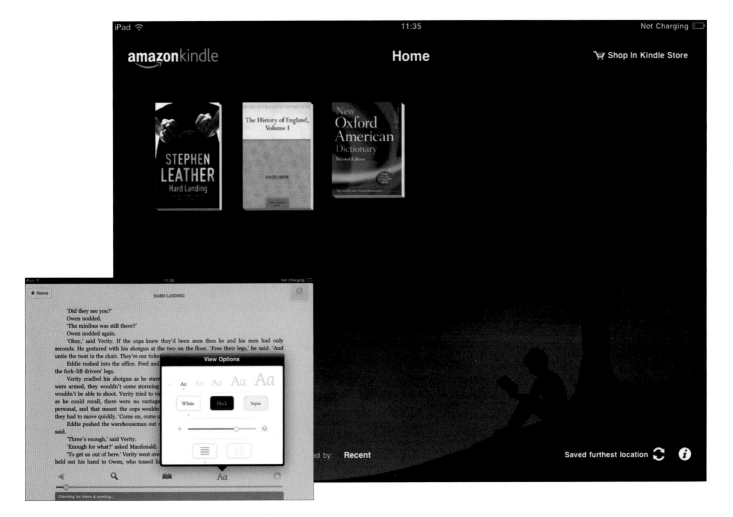

Mocha VNC Lite

Free from *bit.ly/f4X14A*

You didn't know your iPad could run Word or Excel, did you. Well it can... kind of.

Install VNC Lite and you can control any Mac or PC elsewhere on your home or office network, and use the software installed on them as though it were installed on your iPad. Here's how it works.

VNC is a protocol that passes instructions from one device – in this case your iPad – across your network to another computer, and passes back that computer's display to the controller. Set it up in your home and it's the easiest way possible to control a media PC or Mac stationed below your TV without using a regular keyboard or mouse.

If you're worried about the security implications, don't be. Although VNC allows you to open and close applications, create and delete files, send email and shut down the remote machine, it's easy to set up limits on the host that define what the controller can and cannot do when logged in to the system.

Don't let the acronym put you off – this really is a remarkably simple system to set up and, with a wide range of VNC clients to choose from, if you find that this free implementation doesn't meet your growing needs as you get more used to this way of working, you can upgrade over time.

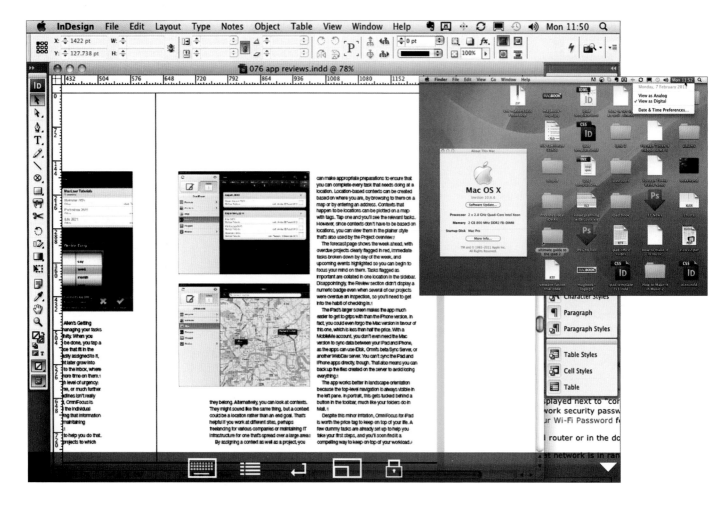

TuneIn Radio

59p from *bit.ly/i4ppDh*

Inexpensive broadband connections have given us greater choice than ever before when it comes to live media. We can now cheaply and easily watch television and listen to radio stations from right around the world from the comfort of our own homes or workplaces.

TuneIn Radio, which works on both the iPad and iPhone, is a comprehensive index of over 40,000 stations worldwide. You can search by station or programme name, programme type, song name and so on.

Search for a station by name and if it appears in the list of possible matches you can tap the drop-down button to the right of its entry and see a timeline of current and future programmes in its schedule. Tapping its icon opens it up in the full screen browser, with controls for playing the feed and details about upcoming content.

It doesn't stop there, though. The control buttons at the bottom of the screen look very much like those on a tape player, and include a record button, allowing you to save the stream to your iPad's

memory for playing back later. You can also schedule recordings for programmes that aren't yet due to be broadcast.

One of the most interesting things about an application like TuneIn Radio is the way in which it lets you explore the global radio landscape and discover new stations.

Once you have found a station you like you can set it as a favourite, which makes it easy to return to later on, or tap the antenna icon at the top of the station's browser page to find other stations that should appeal to anyone who listens to the one to which you're currently tuned.

Returning to the app's home screen, tapping on the Location category calls up a map like the one in the iPad's Maps app, on which station clusters are marked out with push pins. Tapping on them produces a list of broadcasters serving that local area, complete with logos and details of the current programme. If you're looking for local commentary of a football match or other sporting event, this is one of the quickest and easiest ways to follow your team when it's playing away from home.

TuneIn Radio has completely revolutionised the way we think about and listen to the radio, and opened up a new world of listening choices.

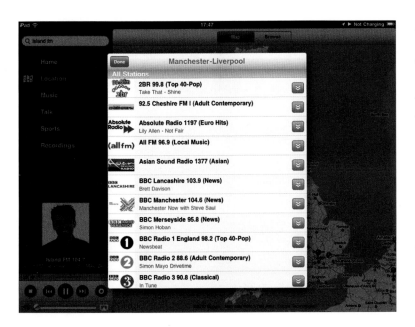

TED
Free from *bit.ly/ecAZNz*

TED stands for Technology, Entertainment, Design. It's a non-profit organisation whose stated aim is to propagate 'ideas worth spreading'. Since 1984, it's gained a significant following among the great and the good of the world, who are practically queueing up to speak at its two annual conferences.

As a non-profit organisation, TED posts fascinating talks online for free, on subjects as diverse as medicine, womens' rights, poetry, sport, the human condition, science, space... and just about any other subject you could imagine.

With the advent of the iPhone and iPad they're now available to iOS users, too, with five new talks popping up every week. There's always something new to watch, and we'd defy you not to find something interesting and engaging to learn.

There are two versions of the app – the regular edition we're using here and a second edition that

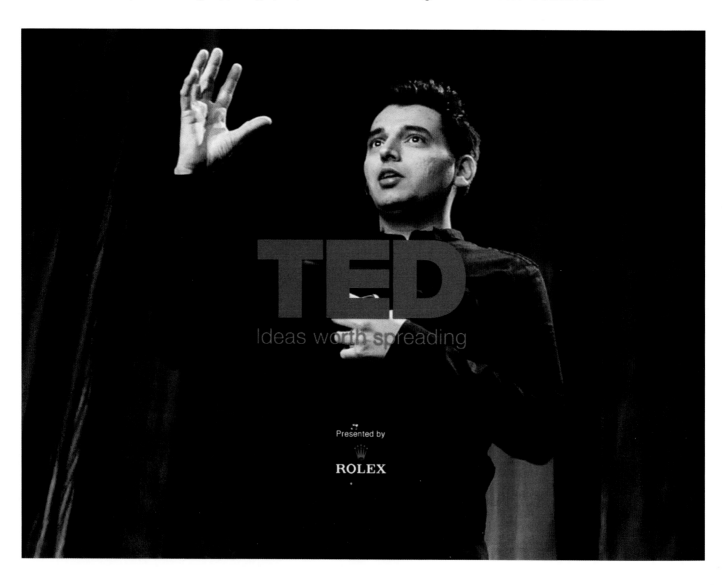

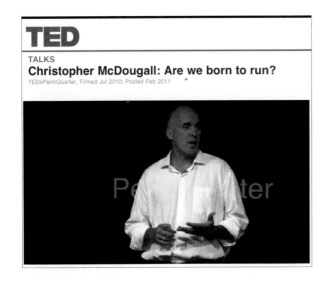

TALKS
Christopher McDougall: Are we born to run?
TEDxPennQuarter, Filmed Jul 2010; Posted Feb 2011

TALKS
Al Gore's new thinking on the climate crisis
TED2008, Filmed Mar 2008; Posted Apr 2008

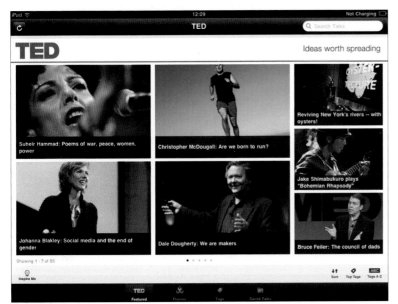

includes subtitles for the hard of hearing. They organise available talks by theme (52 of them) and filters them according to tags (there are 261 at the time of writing).

You can search for specific topics or speakers and save any talks that you want to view when you're away from your wifi connection (we'd not recommend streaming over 3G unless you have a particularly generous contract that won't incur fees for excess use, as this app is addictive).

Our pick of the best speakers and subjects include Apple board member and former US vice president Al Gore, speaking on the subject of climate change, and the Huffington Post's Arianna Huffington on how to succeed. The value of free access to speakers like this is impossible to quantify when you consider how much you might have to pay to hear them speak in person were it not for organisations like TED.

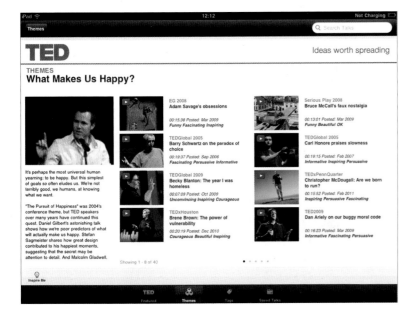

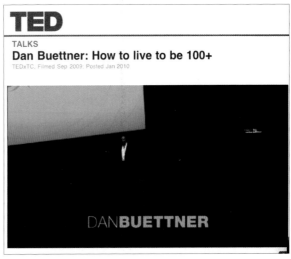

TALKS
Dan Buettner: How to live to be 100+
TEDxTC, Filmed Sep 2009; Posted Jan 2010

iPad games

It may be short of buttons and switches, but the iPad is still a first class gaming device, as these choice apps reveal.

We all know that the iPad's touch-sensitive glass panel is the key to its massive success as a hardware device, but it's only when you use it to play games that you realise what a stroke of brilliance it is.

The iPad may be missing the buttons, switches and joystick controls so important to conventional gaming devices, but it has turned this to its advantage. That glass surface suddenly becomes the largest gaming controller of any console as an ever-expanding range of apps races to take advantage of it. From fast-moving yet unconventional shooters like Angry Birds HD to cerebral classics like Scrabble and Who Wants to be a Millionaire, the iPad is becoming one of the most desirable and best-supported mobile consoles money can buy.

Here we've picked eight of the best games available, concentrating on family classics like Jenga and Worms, alongside classics of the future, such as the phenomenally successful Words With Friends.

However you want to pass your time, you're sure to find something among them to suit your mood.

111   Angry Birds HD

112   Monopoly

113   Who Wants to be a Millionaire

114   Jenga

115   Worms 2: Armageddon

115   Galaxy on Fire 2

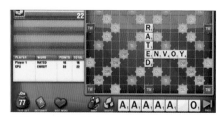

116   Scrabble

117   Words With Friends

Angry Birds HD
£2.99 from *bit.ly/hgfBpH*

Prepare to lose hours of your life to this wonderfully addictive game.

Angry Birds has already earned itself a massive following on the iPhone and iPod touch, and is now doing the same on the iPad. It's easy to see why that is, too.

The premise is simple: an army of snorting, greedy pigs is set on stealing the birds' eggs. You, as the birds' controller, must use the birds' various attributes to fight them off. The trouble is, these birds can't fly without some assistance, and that's where you come in. Each bird hops into a slingshot, and it's up to you to work out the optimum velocity and angle of elevation to bring them crashing down on the pigs, or the barricades that the pigs have built to protect themselves.

The birds come in various colours, sizes and shapes, with each breed given different attributes. The default red bird can do nothing but follow the arc of your trajectory, but the aqua bird can give birth to chicks that drop like cluster bombs, and the yellow bird will put on a spurt of speed when you tap the iPad screen.

It sounds simple. It sounds mundane, but in actual fact it's anything but either of those things. Angry Birds' unfussy, pared down tasks are what make it such a draw, and why it appeals to such a wide range of players.

The skill comes in working out the exact trajectory on which to send each bird to cause the maximum damage to the pigs' defences. This changes from level to level, getting more difficult as the game progresses.

Not only do the pigs get better at barricading themselves, but the materials they use change and becomes stronger. Simple hills are supplemented by fragile glass walls, then planks, blocks and rocks. The pigs aren't bright – they stack blocks and boulders up on top of the upright glass, so if you can score a direct strike on one of the panes you can send the whole lot tumbling. The glass shatters with a satisfying, realistic crash, the rocks fall on the pigs, and they pop. The more pigs you pop, the more you score.

The birds are fragile. As soon as each has been flung from the slingshot it's spent: whether or not they've hit their target each explodes in a feathery puff, but if you have any left at the end of a round that haven't been sent on a doom-laden mission you'll receive bonus points for each one. Points build up quickly, and it's immensely satisfying to see your total tick up by several thousand at a time.

Angry Birds HD is a big game with a lot of levels, but sooner or later you're bound to come to an end, at which point you'll no doubt buy some more courtesy of an in-app purchase.

Monopoly
£5.99 from *bit.ly/dECdKm*

The capitalists' favourite has come to the iPad in the shape of digital Monopoly. This beautiful recreation of the classic board game has given it a welcome breath of new life, staying close to the original and introducing just enough bells and whistles to appeal to those of us who were starting to feel a little bit jaded.

Monopoly is famed for taking hours to play, and that can be reason enough to put off taking out the board, but this iPad edition can be picked up and put down at will and, as well as network multi-player gaming, you can play on your own against the iPad, so if you're the only Monopoly fan in your home you still have a worthy opponent.

The gameplay is much sharper than it is with the board game, allowing you to complete a round in a fraction of the time it otherwise would, and your attention is held by the cute animations. The top hat shoots out stars and currency as it bounces along; the dog gallops playfully; the boot leaves footprints as it leaps ahead. Property, chance and community chest cards pop up as and when needed, so you can see what forfeit or benefit awaits you, and there's no chance of the banker sneakily siphoning off funds to their own pot while you're not looking as the financial side of things is handled by the iPad.

The currency may not be pounds or dollars in this edition – it's a Monopoly invention, of an M struck through by two horizontal lines – but the place names are reassuringly familiar: Bow Street, Leicester Square, Whitehall et al.

If you've never come across Monopoly before or you're not sure how to play the iPad edition then the teacher mode will be your guide. This is more than a how-to on rolling the dice and moving; it also talks strategy. The orange group, for instance, is the most landed-on colour on the board, and Trafalgar Square (red) the most landed on single square, making them excellent properties to own.

iPad Monopoly has given this long-running classic a shot in the arm. We love it.

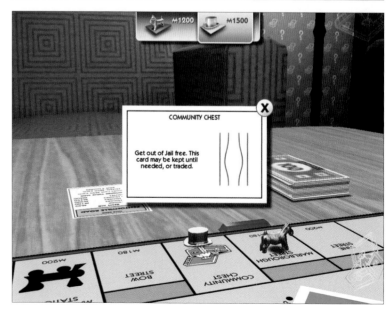

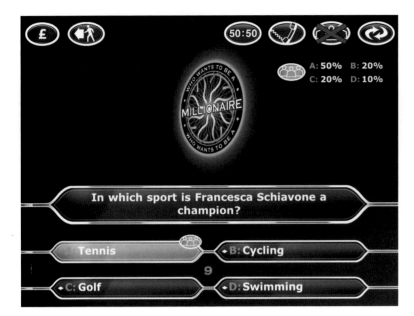

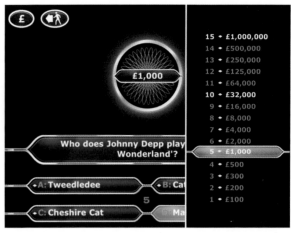

Who Wants To Be a Millionaire

£2.99 from *bit.ly/hQYpth*

As one of the best-known and most-franchised TV shows, Millionaire has earned itself a massive global following. The iPad edition brings much of its excitement to the small screen, with the familiar pulsing music the triumphant stings with every milestone achieved and the stab as you fall back to the last safe position on your first wrong answer.

The questions are graded, getting progressively more difficult as the stakes increase, and as with the

television version you have three lifelines at your disposal: 50:50, phone a friend or ask the audience. You might think this is akin to cheating on a computer game where the iPad already knows the answers, but you shouldn't rely on them to always get you out of a hole. Asking the audience throws up a range of opinions, and when you phone a friend they do sometimes get the answer wrong (although their answers are accompanied by a percentage certainty, so you can make an informed choice about following their advice or not).

There is one further option, and that's to swap out the current question for another. This can only be done once in the game.

As well as the fifteen questions of each game you can optionally play Fastest Finger First, although with no opponents this counts for nothing and you still get through to the game, even if you get them in the wrong order.

It comes with 500 questions, with another 250 available as an in-app purchase for a bargain 59p. Sadly, though, it lacks any kind of scoreboard.

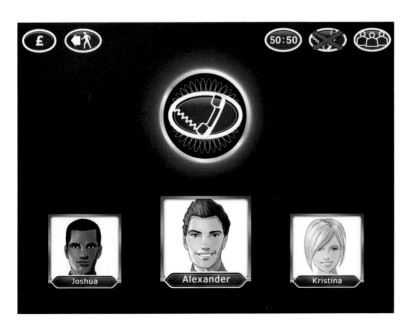

Jenga

59p from *bit.ly/eaGkZU*

You may well wonder how such a tactile game as Jenga translates to the iPad. The answer is: surprisingly well. The iPad is all about touching and swiping, so it's perhaps the best platform going for a game like this.

If you've never played before, the idea is simple. A tower of blocks is set up on the table. Your job is to make it taller, but without any other blocks in play the only way you can do this is by taking out a bricks from lower down the stack and putting it onto the top. With three bricks in every level it's not long before the weights and balances start to change, some blocks become trickier to remove and start to tug on those above them, and as you pull you start to tug at the integrity of the structure until eventually... inevitably... the whole tower comes tumbling down. If you're the player who was touching the blocks when it happened, you're out.

Unlike the physical table-top game, though, you haven't spoiled it for everyone else, as although your game is brought to an end, the other players in your group can carry on as the tower is rebuilt into its last good state.

The game's 3D engine is great, and key to its success, allowing you to move yourself up and down and around the stack to get a better view of the contact points between each brick. Without it, you'd find it close to impossible to play.

The replay opportunities of the classic game where all the bricks are the same colour are fairly low, even if you opt for pass and play where you pass the iPad between a group of friends as you each take your turn, but the arcade variant has much greater potential. Here you're playing against the clock, and you earn bonuses for matching the variously coloured bricks as you stack them on the top of the tower. These bonuses can be used to buy cheats such as extra time or the ability to count a brick as any colour you want. Even so, you'll have to be very good to get on the high score board.

Worms 2: Armageddon

£2.99 from *bit.ly/eYgNeQ*

Atten-shun! Fall in line. It's time to head out onto the battlefield for some wacky turn-based warfare. Pick a weapon from a massive and varied arsenal including homing missiles, the Holy hand grenade and exploding sheep, then deliver a painful payload to your enemies. Your team of four filthy worms has a simple objective: be the last one standing.

Once you've moved a single worm, the baton is passed to another team to unleash sweet vengeance. Worms isn't all about the big guns, though. There's plenty of its vicious humour. An enemy worm that's precariously vulnerable atop a cliff is just asking to be given a nudge with a baseball bat. Even funnier hijinks occur when an attack goes wrong and sends a land mine hurtling back to the would-be victor.

Worms 2 adds additional game modes and new weapons, but its most significant improvement is multi-player, which lets you play against up to three people over Bluetooth or one over the Internet on wifi; 3G isn't supported. Unlike the original, this is a universal app, so you can play on your iPad against your kids on their iPod touch for the cost of one app.

Galaxy on Fire 2

£5.99 from *bit.ly/grDqpf*

Bounty hunter Keith Maxwell is tasked with tracking down a trio of rogues, but even a man of his skills can't prepare for what follows. During the dogfight that opens Galaxy on Fire 2, his ship's hyperdrive is damaged. Upon engaging it, he's flung to a remote sector of the galaxy. Much worse, it transpires that the diversion has also flung him through time.

Faced with a very different political map, Maxwell starts afresh with a bucket of bolts to earn a living by mining asteroids, ferrying passengers, and hunting scum and villainy. His journey home won't be easy, as he's given ominous warning about a vicious race, the Void, that's on the prowl.

Graphics are competent and atmospheric, although ship models aren't exactly attractive. Mining missions are fleshed out as mini-games in which you have to steady the drill head until you've bled the core dry. Dogfights are tense and challenging, but it's easy to work out the relative positions of enemies. Matters are simplified by auto-fire and your ship's constant velocity.

In all, Galaxy on Fire 2 is a portable success that you can easily dip in and out of.

Scrabble for iPad

£3.99 from bit.ly/elpalQ

We've compared many of the games here to their analogue equivalents, commenting on how well they make the transition to the iPad. With Scrabble, it's a triumph: this is better than the real thing.

The board looks beautiful, the fact that the tiles don't quite line up gives them added realism, and the noise they make as you drop them onto the board is great. There's a built-in dictionary so you can check the validity (it understands both color and colour; ax and axe; neighbor and neighbour...) and a sneaky 'Best Word' button. Tap this and the iPad will analyse your letters and the make-up of the board, and move tiles from your rack into the game in the position where they'll achieve the highest possible score. It's unlikely you'd be able to bag yourself a better mark, but if you don't want to follow its suggestion you can recall the tiles to your rack, although you'll still have used up one of your four possible Best Word attempts.

In many ways, Scrabble is a better game than Words With Friends. The letter distribution is the same as it is for the physical board game, and the layout's the same, too, with the bonus squares in their familiar places; more of your friends will be familiar with traditional Scrabble if you're playing together.

You can play as a group by passing the iPad between each other, or play multi-player over a local network using a variety of iPads, iPhones and iPod touches. There's also a neat Party Play option, which hooks in to a free Tile Rack application that can be downloaded from the App Store. This keeps your tiles on your local iPhone or iPod touch while the board game is displayed on the iPad. Each player flicks tiles from the Rack onto the iPad, and there arranges them on the board. In this way, you'll keep your tiles in private view while your opponents are taking their turn, and can use a local dictionary to check combinations. Smartly, the iPad board remembers where each player is sitting and rotates on each turn to face them.

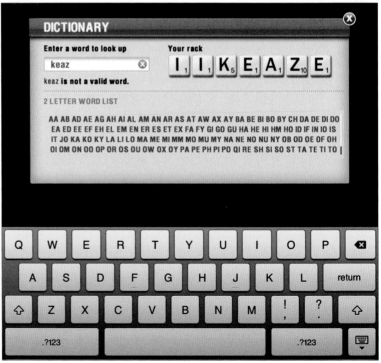

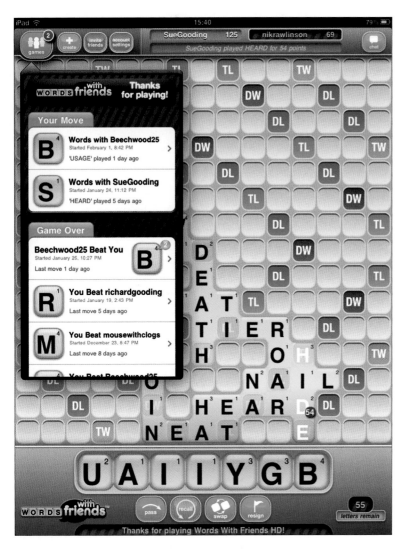

Words With Friends
£1.79 from bit.ly/gcEyq9

Words with Friends is Scrabble's main competitor, and it's not difficult to see why: it has one killer feature in the form of Internet connectivity. Where Scrabble relies on a local home or office network for multi-player, multi-device gaming, Words With Friends will happily connect you over the Internet with anyone else who happens to have it installed, whether they be using an iPad, an iPhone or an iPod touch.

Unlike Scrabble it's a portrait-only game, played with your board at the top of the screen and the tile rack below. You can zoom in very slightly, but unlike the iPod touch / iPhone version where zooming really is required (and indeed automatic when you start dropping tiles on the board) the iPad's screen is large enough to manage without.

If you're running it on several devices you'll need to create an account with New Toy, the game's creator. This is free and is used to synchronise your moves and racks across each device so that you can pick up on your iPad where you leave off on your iPhone and vice versa. Games are organised within a drop-down menu on the toolbar.

The toolbar is also the place to look if you want to taunt your opponents. Because Words With Friends isn't designed specifically for playing with someone else in the same room (as Scrabble is), there's a built-in chat system which, as with the board and racks, is also synchronised across as many devices as are logged in to your account.

In many ways it's easier to rack up higher score with Words With Friends than it is with Scrabble thanks to the more generous distribution of bonus tiles. As with Scrabble they encompass double and triple word scores, and double and triple letter cells, but because the triple word bonuses have been moved in from the corners they're easier to hit with multiple words, which can run through them, even at the top and bottom of the board.

For local gaming, then, pick Scrabble. For remote, it's Words With Friends all the way.

Parental Controls

The iPad is a great educational tool, and kids will take quickly to its tactile touch, sweep and pinch way of working. That's all the more reason for you to consider how to keep them safe when using the App Store and other downloaded content.

Apple has been slightly inconsistent when it comes to tailoring the specific abilities and content of an iPad, iPhone and iPod touch. If you want to keep your children away from content you feel is inappropriate for them, you should turn to Parental Controls in iTunes' Preferences (right), and to Restrictions on the iPad (Home screen > Settings > General > Restrictions). Both of these let you exert increasing levels of control over what can be downloaded and installed, until you get to the point where you're happy allowing younger users to get their hands on your iPad.

To invoke restrictions on your iPad, tap Enable Restrictions and choose a four-digit security code (below). This must be entered when making any changes to your settings, and it so should stop your children disabling them. Once restrictions are enabled you can disable whole applications, such

as Safari, YouTube and iTunes, forbid App Store installations (1) and switch off the location features.

Ratings can be tailored for specific territories, with options for Australia, Canada, France, Germany, Ireland, Japan, New Zealand, the UK and the US (2). Choosing your home territory will let you pick from restrictions that match your local ratings. So, pick UK and you'll have movie ratings of U, Uc, PG, 12, 12A, 15 and 18. Switch to Ireland, though, and you'll be able to choose from G, PG, 12, 15, 16 and 18 (3). Likewise, in the UK you can allow all or no TV shows, or just those rated for 'Caution' (4). In the US, though, you have 16 ratings from TV-Y to TV-MA. In all countries, the choices for podcasts are simply on or off for explicit content (5), but the options for applications are more extensive and match Apple's own App Store ratings system (6).

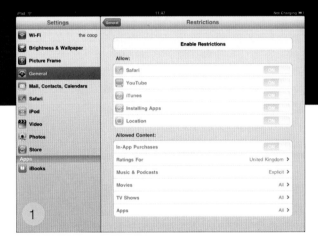

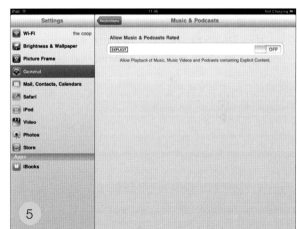

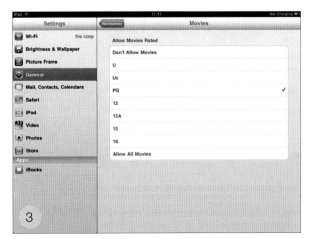

iPad in iTunes

iTunes is more than just a music playing, app-downloading tool on your Mac or PC – it's the main conduit through which you'll configure your iPad. Here's we examine its most important features.

Like the iPhone and iPod, the iPad interfaces with your Mac or PC through iTunes. This application, whose name is becoming more inappropriate and limiting by the day, not only loads music and movies onto the iPad, but also draws down data from the applications you've been using on the device itself so that you can back it up on your computer, and use it there in other applications.

Plug it in using the bundled connector cable and it will appear in iTunes' sidebar while your USB port charges its battery. You can plug it in to a powered USB hub, too, but you won't always find that this charges the battery, so keep an eye on your power.

Clicking the iPad in the sidebar opens up the tabbed configuration panel through which you manage its settings and content. At the bottom of the screen you'll also see a capacity bar showing how much of your available space you've used up (and it's colour-coded to show you what makes up those contents) and a Sync button that uploads content from your Mac or PC to your iPad and downloads any content you bought on the iPad itself so that you won't lose it if you have a problem with your device.

Clicking through the tabs should be enough for you to work out what you can do on each one, with Apps perhaps the most important. This not only lets you upload applications you have bought from the iTunes Store onto your iPad, but it also allows you to organise where they sit on the various home screens (see right).

The same page is also where you download content you have created on the iPad using third-party apps through File Sharing (see below right).

This feature comes with the caveat that not all files can be downloaded natively. If you have installed Pages, Keynote and Numbers from the iWork suite you won't see any of their native files, even on a Mac with the full edition of iWork installed. To download your work from these applications you must first convert by using the Export option inside each application. When you do, they'll appear in the File Sharing dialogue.

The process works both ways, so if you've created files using the equivalent applications on

Above: iTunes remains the only officially-supported means of synchronising all of the data and applications on your iPad with your PC or Mac. Use this to choose which applications should be stored on your iPad, and to organise the screens on which they appear without having to manually drag them from screen to screen on the iPad itself.

your Mac you can upload them to the iPad through File Sharing and they'll be available to read and edit on the move.

Sadly there isn't, currently, any official way to synchronise your iPad to your Mac or PC wirelessly over your local network or 3G connection. However, some utilities such as Dropbox and SugarSync will let you synchronise data using online servers, with the results reflected on each of the machines on which the application is installed – including your iPad. Until Apple adds this feature to an iOS update or authorises a third-part application onto the App Store to perform such wholesale wireless synchronisation, though, there remains no way to synchronise your iTunes library, movies, TV shows and apps without using iTunes and USB.

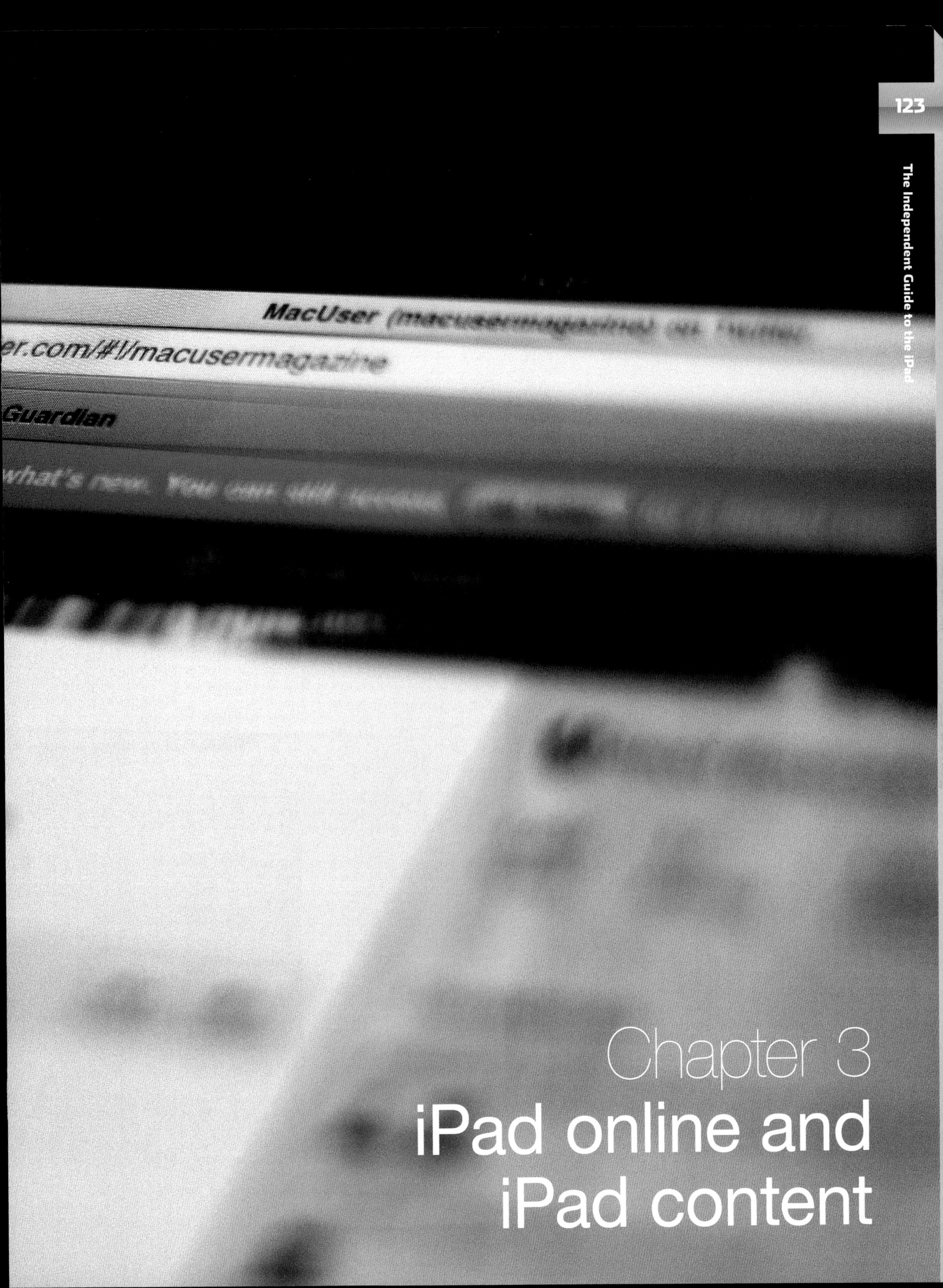

MacUser

er.com/#!/macusermagazine

Guardian

Chapter 3
iPad online and
iPad content

The Independent Guide to the iPad

Getting social

With an iPad in your bag, you can keep in touch with friends, family and business colleagues on the major social networks at any time of the day, wherever you happen to be.

Twitter

Free from *bit.ly/blhxRh*

Twitter is the social network everyone's talking about... and indeed the social network on which everyone is talking. From not-so-humble beginnings it has attracted a global following that stretches to many millions. It's the darling of film and music stars, TV shows, radio station and anyone else who wants to get their message out to the world.

The vast majority of its members, though, are regular users like you and me who use the service to follow our favourite celebrities and keep in touch with friends and family.

There's a wide choice of iPad Twitter applications to choose from, and here we recommend two: the official Twitter application and, overleaf, TweetDeck.

The Twitter app takes a little getting used to, but when you've got your head around its sliding panels it's logical and easy to use. On the very left of the screen you have six main sections, which hold three types of Tweet – Timeline, Mentions and direct Messages addressed specifically to you – as well as user lists, your profile information and a search tool for finding specific information. Tapping any one of them opens up its contents to the right. Tapping a link in those contents, a user name, a mention and so on, goes on to open that content, again to the right, sliding off the existing content to the left. To continue exploring, simply keep clicking and sliding.

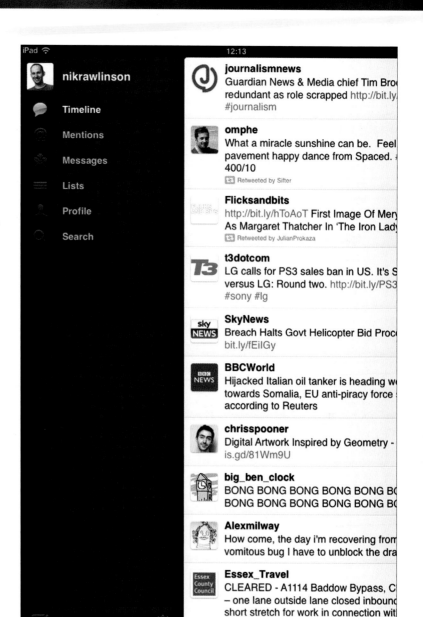

How to find Twitter accounts you want to follow

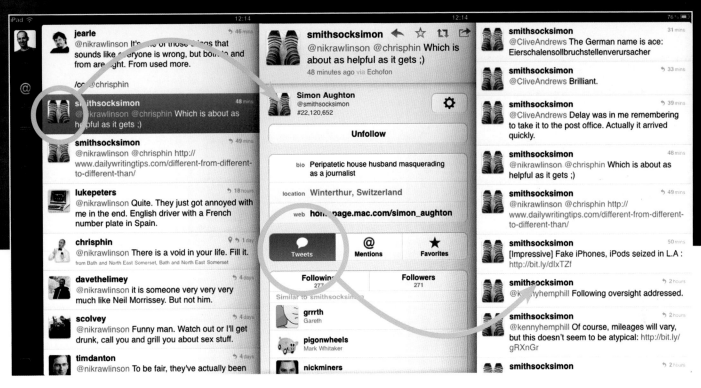

Tap the Twitter member's icon. This calls up their profile, showing you a short biography, their followers and who they're following. It may include a location and web link, depending on how much info they've chosen to share through their profile.

The Favourites button lists Tweets they've chosen to save, while Mention lists those tweets from other Twitter members that mention or are publicly directed at this user. To read this particular user's own contributions to the Twitter network, tap Tweets.

You can now see a list of all of their Tweets in reverse chronological order. Tapping any of the names they mention (preceded by @) lets you repeat the process with those people, helping you find more Twitter members that you may want to add to the list of people you're following.

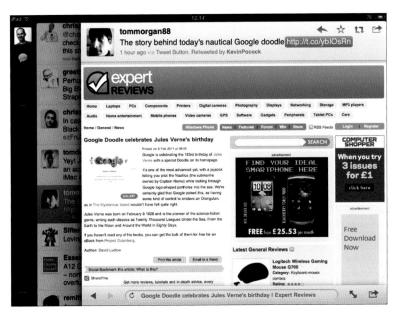

How to open linked web pages

There's no need to copy a Tweeted link and paste it into Safari, as Twitter can use the iPad's built-in browser tools to render pages within its own interface. Tap a link and a new pane slides in from the right to display the page in question, with the original tweet shown in a strip above.

Twitter is intelligent enough to tailor the pane size to match its content, so if the link was to an image hosted on one of the most common Twitter image hosting services, such as Yfrog or Twitpic, it will open a smaller window, leaving more of the original Twitter stream visible in the left-hand half of the application window.

TweetDeck
Free from *bit.ly/ahHdYX*

TweetDeck has a more conventional interface than Twitter, but still benefits from a certain amount of swiping and tapping to make best use of the iPad's limited screen space.

Hold it in portrait orientation and every Tweet you tap in the columns that fill the lower portion of the interface will be opened as a speech bubble in the space above (see grab, below left). If you tap a web link in a tweet that, too, opens as a preview in the pane at the top of the app, and can be sent to Safari with a single tap (below right). Turning the iPad to landscape orientation dispenses with the panel, flipping around the whole application window when you click on a link to display it full screen.

Anyone who has used the regular desktop-based version of TweetDeck knows that its power lies in the multiple columns that can be stacked up side by side in direct contrast to the Twitter app's use of a categorised list of message types. This lets you keep an eye on several accounts simultaneously without having to switch between them.

By adding more than one Twitter account through the app settings you can display the streams from each one side by side. You can also post to multiple accounts at once, as tapping the new tweet button when you have more than one account set up calls up the regular entry pane topped by a button for each of your accounts. Tapping them turns them on and off and thus specifies which accounts should receive the tweet you're writing.

This feature alone makes TweetDesk much more powerful than Twitter for those with multiple accounts, and there are other features in the works. Unlike the desktop edition of the app, this version of TweetDeck for iPad works only with Twitter, but Facebook integration is promised for version 2.

HootSuite

Free from bit.ly/dMmlfb

HootSuite represents the pinnacle of social posting for both Twitter and Facebook accounts, even letting you forward-date your Tweets and Facebook jottings.

This forward-dating feature is a real boon for anyone who uses social networking tools in a business context, allowing them to stack up a list of potential posts and set them all live at regular intervals – even when they're not able to get to the app to maintain a constant, measured presence.

Like TweetDeck, it presents your various streams in columns that spread out across the screen and can be swiped both horizontally, and vertically. If you have several accounts registered with the app then they'll all appear in the left-hand column. Linked Twitter images and web pages appear within a browser window inside the app itself, which slides up from the bottom of the window. Images posted to Facebook appear as thumbnails in a floating dialogue.

If you use both Facebook and Twitter on the iPad then this is, without question, our number one choice for using the two side by side.

How to forward-date your postings

Select the account from which you want to make a posting and press the new post button (a square with a pen pointing towards its centre). Write your post in the usual way and tap the account icons at the top left of the dialogue to choose which ones should punt the update out to their followers. Now tap the Schedule icon at the bottom of the dialogue and use the tumblers to choose a date and time to make the posting live, to within five minutes.

Friendly
Free from *bit.ly/ieWHyU*

It has an official app for iPhone users, but Facebook hasn't yet come out with an equivalent for the iPad. Moreover, the site is so extensive and contains such varied content that we perhaps shouldn't be entirely surprised that the choice of fully-featured Facebook apps on the app store is slim to say the least.

There are plenty that offer a subset of Facebook features, such as photo viewing and, as we've already seen, you can post and read text content

using Hootsuite and, if the promises for version 2 play out, TweetDeck, but few other than Friendly replicate almost every aspect of the site in a unified app-based interface.

Sadly some parts do throw you out to a browser window of its own. Tap the downward arrow on the Live Feed tab (see image, left) and you'll find links to all of Facebook's key tools, including photos, links and videos. Tapping them spins the app around to show them in a regular Facebook web view, with a Done button added to the browser's toolbar that flips you back to the app when tapped.

Likewise, if you need to access Facebook-linked apps like Farmville or Scrabble worldwide then these, too, are beyond the realm of this application.

There are benefits to using Friendly, though, chief among them being the fact that you can leave it running in the background while using Safari for regular browsing. Further, by switching to an app rather than using a browser to access Facebook, you do lose all of the margin advertising, although as we're using the free edition (ad-free Facely Plus is just 59p) it is itself ad-supported, with small banners running across the bottom.

How to comment on a post

Half the fun of Facebook is the interaction between users. If you couldn't comment on your friends' postings and photos you wouldn't spend nearly so long on the site.

Athough Friendly punts you out to a captive version of the browser to comment on photos, it's very easy to use it to comment on a regular posting, as seen here. Tapping the comments link immediately below the post opens up the message thread with an entry box immediately below it (see left). Type your message and tap Post to set it live, just as you would on Facebook itself.

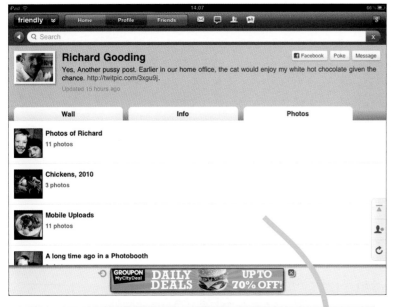

How to find Facebook photos

Facebook provides its users with one of the best online photo galleries currently available, and Friendly makes it even better.

Find a user's albums by clicking the Photos tab in their profile, which presents them all as a list (top left). Tapping an album's name opens it up, with all of its contents displayed as thumbnails (centre left). If they spread over more than one screen you'll see a page count at the top of the screen, and can switch between them using the arrows to the left and right of the screen.

Tapping on an image opens it full screen and overlays it with any caption set by the album's owner (bottom left).

The speech bubbles on each photo and the galleries themselves let you add comments, although this is done through a regular browser window.

Two Friendly alternatives

Facebook touch / *bit.ly/gDg7R1*

Invest 59p and you can bag a copy of Facebook touch, which adds several features to the free Friendly's abilities, including native photo commenting and customisable themes, but still no access to Facebook applications within the app.

Facepad / *bit.ly/fdM7ne*

Facepad cleverly presents the body of Facebook's native browser-based pages, wrapped up inside an app interface. A menu running down the left-hand side of the screen gives you quick access to Groups, Friends, Messages and so on, again letting you leaving this active in the background while you do other things with your browser.

Free content

What would the iPad be without great applications and first-rate content to use with them? The Internet is fit to burst with high quality media, much of which can be yours for free... legally.

Music

Before the iTunes Music Store came along, it was practically impossible to legally download music: the major record companies simply didn't make it available. Out of that frustration grew alternatives such as the original Napster sharing service, which allowed you to freely (but illegally) swap your music collection with other users across the Internet.

Naturally, the record companies didn't like this much, and so they took legal action, ending the era of free-for-all downloading. Then came Apple's store, offering music from major artists for less than the price of the CD version. Now also offering TV series' and podcasts, it's still one of the best ways of filling up your iPod, with over half of UK music downloads now coming from here alone.

Although the original Napster is long gone, replaced by a legally compliant store of the same name, it's still possible to find plenty of free media online, legally, and without having to install complex programs. You may have to hunt around a little, but there are all sorts of hidden gems just waiting to be discovered – here's the inside track.

ARTIST HOMEPAGES

If there's a particular artist that you're fond of, take a good look around their official website, which you should find easily enough through a search engine such as Google (*google.co.uk*). You can often hear a low-quality streaming version of their music, but

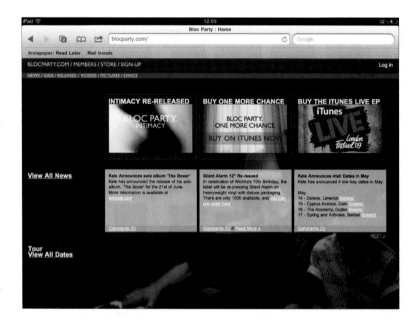

you might also come across anything from promo videos and interviews, to MP3 files that you can save into your iTunes folder and transfer to your iPod.

You may also have to register first, by giving your email address and providing a username, but it's worth persevering to get to the 'inner sanctum' of these sites. It's often the first place you'll find previews of a new single, and it's also a great way to get hold of exclusive, previously unheard or live material. A browse around the Internet reveals all kinds of free downloads.

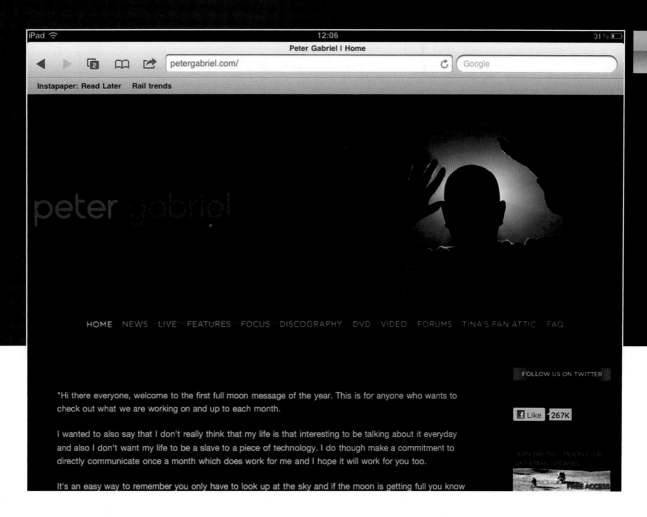

Bloc Party *blocparty.com*
Live, studio and demo tracks from the music press darlings of 2005. Also links to 'The Marshals' fan site, which offers further, unreleased material.

Elvis Costello *elviscostello.com*
Audio interviews in WMA format, where the master songsmith discusses his approach to writing. iTunes is capable of converting WMA tracks to iPod friendly formats.

Jamie Cullum *jamiecullum.com*
Jazz pianist and singer and BBC Radio 2 specialist music presenter's homepage, offering unreleased live tracks.

Oasis *oasisnet.com*
Sign up to the BritPop survivors' official site to gain access to exclusive tracks, plus a streaming 'Radio Supernova' playing back-to-back Oasis hits.

Peter Gabriel *petergabriel.com*
Register for the 'Full Moon Club' and get access to exclusive tracks.

Sigur Ròs *sigur-ros.co.uk*
A generous selection of unreleased live and studio tracks from the site of the Icelandic shoe-gazers.

RECORD COMPANIES
With the Internet's potential to promote and distribute music, record companies are feeling more nervous than ever about their role. As such, many are recasting themselves as front-line champions of new music, as well as guardians of artists' back catalogues.

Matador Records *matadorrecords.com*
From the label that houses indie-alternative notaries such as Interpol and Cat Power, a fine collection of unreleased and new artist tracks. Follow the links on the front page for new album teaser tracks in their entirety, as well as videos of interviews and live performances.

Subpop *subpop.com*
Indie label with names such as Nirvana, The Afghan Whigs and Saint Etienne on its books. The Media link will take you to a page offering free downloads of individual tracks from established artists, as well

as new signings. You can also subscribe to podcasts, which can be set to automatically download into iTunes when they're updated.

Rykodisc *rykodisc.com*
Long-running label with an extensive high-profile back catalogue. Go to the See and Hear Music section to find free artist-themed Podcasts, including some excellent interviews and album previews.

Victory Records *victoryrecords.com*
US-based rock label with a sizeable collection of good-quality MP3 downloads and streams in the Media section.

Kill Rock Stars *killrockstars.com*
A US label that has nurtured alternative folk heroes such as Elliot Smith and The Decemberists. Scroll down the page for a substantial archive of free music and video downloads.

UNSIGNED ARTISTS
It's not just signed artists who are keen to have you cramming their music onto your iPod. The Internet was hailed as a revolution for unsigned bands, as it took the means of distribution away from the major labels and put it into the hands of everyone. This has worked out well for the artists, and even better for the music enthusiast: a few leisurely clicks of your mouse can put you in touch with bands on the other side of the world. With so much competition out there, artists are also less precious about charging for their labours and many are happy to give away their music for the price of a listen.

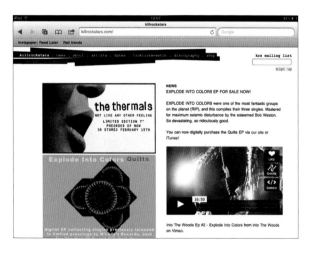

If you're feeling adventurous, we would recommend you start by heading to music-related online communities, where you'll find the homepages of countless artists looking for your attention.

Alternatively, there are more formalised sites that offer editorial content to help you narrow down the choice to your own tastes. Ultimately, there's no quality control other than your own ears, but that's all part of the attraction.

MySpace *myspace.com*
A general-interest online community and social-networking site, but with a particularly good music section. A good touch is the built-in music player that kicks in as soon as you land on a homepage. If you like what you hear, download the track. If not, move on. Not all artists will let you download full versions of their tracks, but the number of signed bands who have a presence here is an encouraging sign.

GarageBand *garageband.com*
A great place to start, with no less than ex-Beatles producer George Martin waxing lyrical over its standards. The structure can be a little confusing, but there are plenty of artists and bands to choose from, all organised by genre. Head for the artists' pages rather than the song links, as you can then see immediately whether or not there's a Download MP3 link.

IUMA *iuma.com*

Ad-supported online community for unsigned bands. Easily navigated and generally fuss-free, offering thousands of downloads by genre, as well as a featured-artists section and lively online forums.

Unsigned Bands *unsignedbandweb.com*

Another welcoming community for those artists and bands looking for an audience. Some slightly rough edges to the site are made up for by a choice of several streaming web-based radio stations showcasing new talent, active forums and a broad selection of genres.

REVIEW SITES

You don't have to rely on Rolling Stone or NME to get your music news any more. There's a whole wealth of online review sites, music magazines and blogs, many of which also have links to free music.

Epitonic *epitonic.com*

Describing itself as 'your source of cutting-edge music', this magazine site offers a healthy complement of editorial, as well as a whole stack of high-quality downloads. There's also the Black Box feature, which allows you to log in and play your favourite tracks from anywhere. Mainly contemporary material.

Pitchfork Media *pitchforkmedia.com*

A review site aimed at picking out the crop of current releases, dwelling mostly on urban, alternative and indie-rock. The editorial and free MP3 downloads are variable in quality, but it's up to date and rarely sits on the fence.

Into Music *intomusic.co.uk*

An excellent combination of music magazine and download service. There are nominal fees to gain access to the music of signed bands, but many of the lesser-known and unsigned artists are offering free downloads.

PeopleSound *peoplesound.com*

Combining signed and unsigned artists. Once you've registered, you can download or stream from thousands of tracks, as well as build up playlists of your favourites that can be accessed and listened to from any computer.

Giga Tracks *gigatracks.com*

An excellent site offering hand-picked selections of new music from unsigned artists, each accompanied by a considered review. You'll also find relevant industry news and features.

Classic Cat *classiccat.net*

An exhaustive catalogue of links to freely downloadable classical music, organised by composer. It can take a while to navigate to external sites to actually download the tracks, but it's worth it for the sheer amount of music on offer.

MUSIC STORES

Amazon *amazon.com*

It may seem an odd gesture for the online retailing giant to give away its goods, but that's what it's currently doing with album tracks from featured artists, as well as lesser-known music. Make sure you're using the US (.com) version of the site and follow the 'free downloads' link hiding on the top right of the Music section, then log in to download the MP3s.

CNET Downloads *http://music.download.com*

Huge number of free music downloads from the equally huge CNET Empire, covering both unsigned and, increasingly, signed artists. Most offer at least one free track. A wide-ranging selection, including a number of spoken word, comedy and children's.

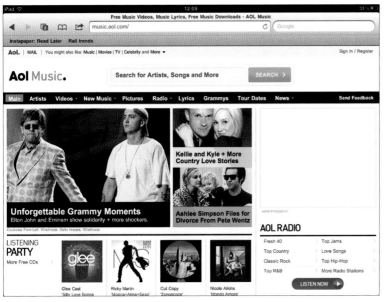

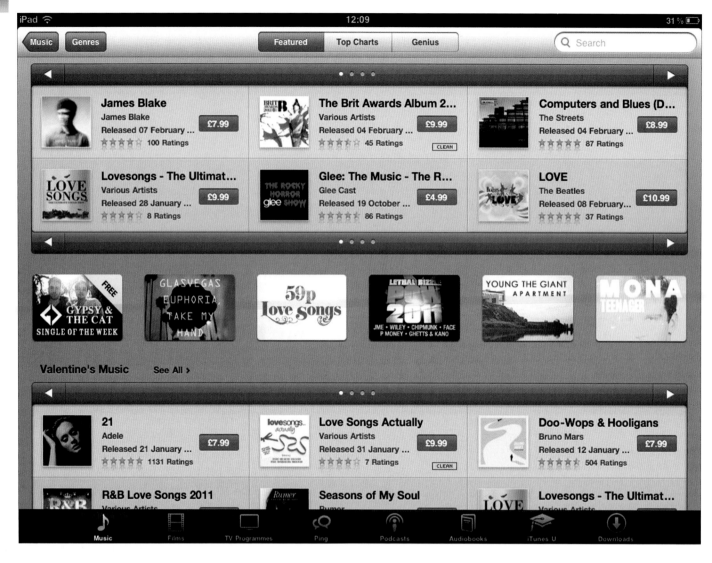

AOL *http://music.aol.com*

Dozens of free downloads from high-profile contemporary artists. Just be aware that when you download a track, the email address you provide is passed on to the band's record company (although it's easily fooled), and you'll be automatically signed up for the AOL newsletter, too. Go to the Songs menu to find the download links.

iTunes Music Store via the iTunes Player

Not to be left out, even Apple's own store offers free downloads. These can generally be found advertised subtly at the bottom right-hand corner of the store's front page, and are generally updated every Tuesday. They also appear on the iPad version, roughly half way down the page.

It's also worth signing up for updates from Apple and other outlets to be kept abreast of new content appearing on their stores.

PUBLIC DOMAIN

Under current UK law, the copyright on a piece of music lasts 70 years from the end of the year of the author's death, and 50 years for the recording itself. After that, copyright ceases, and it passes in to the public domain. So, a recording of Mozart's *Requiem Mass* recorded last year will still be under copyright, but one recorded in 1935 or before won't be.

The BBC used this to good effect with its Beethoven season in 2005, offering free downloads on its website, followed by a similar season of Bach. Using music recorded by its own orchestra, it could forgo paying extra royalties. More of these are planned in the future, so keep an eye on *bbc.co.uk/music*.

Naturally, it's generally older and mostly classical music that's going to be available in this way, but as major libraries around the world begin to put their archives online, expect to find all sorts of interesting examples appearing.

Public Domain 4 U *http://publicdomain4u.com*
A fascinating archive of public domain music, with a strong focus on early 20th century roots music, and no need to register.

The Piano Society *pianosociety.com*
A site for professional and amateur pianists to showcase their talent, the best are picked and given away as free MP3s. More than 50 classical composers are represented, making this a great way to find high-quality and well-recorded piano music. There is also plenty of educational information about both the track and its author.

Creative Commons *http://creativecommons.org/*
Creative Commons is a relatively new form of copyright declaration that allows artists to prescribe exactly what can and can't be done with their online creations. There are six basic types of licence, plus more specialised versions, but most allow the download of work at least for personal use. Go to *http://creativecommons.org/wired* to find an entire album of high-profile artists who got together with Wired magazine to produce an album that can be used for anything except advertising other products. There's also a special Google search engine built into the site, so you can scour the rest of the Internet for Creative Commons licensed works.

CCMixter *http://ccmixter.org*
This site hosts a huge number of samples and remixes derived from work licensed under the Creative Commons licensing scheme, which are themselves subject to the same copyright freedoms. Submission is open to all, but the quality is nonetheless excellent – a great example of how the scheme is changing music distribution.

Free Kids Music *http://freekidsmusic.com*
An American site offering music geared towards children. It's not all of great artistic merit, and contains a lot of links to adverts, but you'll find enough here to keep the kids amused for a while.

Books

Of course, it's not just music that you can find for free online. The App Store is fit to burst with free applications and, if you know where to look, there are plenty of free books on the net, too. To save you the chore of hunting them down, here is a selection of the best.

Project Gutenberg *http://gutenberg.org*
Project Gutenberg has long been the first place to turn if you want to download free books. It was established in 1971 by Michael Hart with the aim of digitising the 10,000 most consulted books by the end of the 20th century, and making them available to the public at little or no charge at all.

The first document to be digitised was the United States declaration of Independence, which has now been joined by over 34,000 other books and documents.

A non-profit corporation, Project Gutenberg is US-based, but its content is global in scope. On average 50 new e-books are added to its library each week, so even if the volume you'd like to read isn't yet there, there's a chance it could be soon. Neither is Project Gutenberg a purely English-language enterprise, with French, German, Finish, Dutch, Portuguese and Chinese particularly well represented.

Don't go there expecting to download the latest Jilly Cooper or the Steig Larsson *Millennium* trilogy any time soon: all books included in the archive are out of copyright, and so you won't find modern titles among them. However, if you feel the need to catch up with the classics then you will find a hugely extensive selection to pick from.

Project Gutenberg is largely run by volunteers, who each work on titles of interest to them and post them to the site. Over the years, the range of formats in which books have been available has grown, from plain text and HTML to now include ePub both with and without images, Kindle format, again with and without images, Plucker and QiOO Mobile. If you are downloading books to read on your iPad then you should opt for one of the two

ePub formats as these can be handled natively by the iBooks app.

You are free to pass on any of the books that you download from Project Gutenberg, and those to whom you give them can do the same, as the project's goal extends to making electronic books as widely available as possible.

The best place to start looking for a book to read is the most of 100 most popular downloads. Visit

Subscription services

The Internet has caused all sorts of headaches for those concerned with intellectual property, but it's even more confusing for the consumer. There was a time when you bought a CD and could pretty much do whatever you wanted with it, but the album you've just bought from the Internet doesn't physically exist.

That's led to a new model of subscription services, whereby for a set amount of money each month you can effectively 'rent' a music collection, which you lose the right to play should you cancel your subscription. Sadly, although it has been adopted by high-profile names including Napster, HMV and Virgin, none of these services are compatible with the iPod – something that's not clear until you trawl through the small print. Apple itself has in the past publicly said it has no plans to offer such a service.

There are, however, a couple of companies that allow you to download tracks for a set monthly fee. If you buy more than an album or two a month, even from iTunes, these services can work out a lot cheaper.

Wippit *wippit.com*
Wippit has 600,000 recordings from 200 record labels, and also has a hefty classical music section, as well as a free downloads area for non-subscribers.

You'll then get unlimited access to the library, which is regularly rotated, so you're guaranteed a fresh supply. All the other music on the site is available at a discounted 'subscribers rate',

which varies by track. Unfortunately, there's not a huge amount currently available in an iPod-compatible MP3 format, so to avoid disappointment, make sure you use the advanced filter to only show these.

eMusic *emusic.com*
Going to the homepage of this subscription site it will immediately ask you to subscribe – even the 14-day free trial requires you to enter your credit card details before you get any more information. Don't let that put you off, though – you can bypass this to check out the site by going directly to *emusic.com/browse/all.html*. You can also cancel your subscription before the end of the free period. If you do, not only will you not be charged, but you'll also be able to keep any tracks you've downloaded.

Three levels of monthly subscription are available. There's no minimum sign-up period, and you can keep the tracks if your subscription lapses. A great-value option.

Spotify *spotify.com*
The current darling of streamed music services offers a subscription service that allows you to download tracks to a portable player and also streams its massive library without the frequent ads that interrupt the listening experience of non-paying users.

It's not yet available in the US, but keep an eye out as that could change any time, at which point it's well worth signing up.

gutenberg.org and click Top downloads on the bar that runs across the top of the page. This will initially present you with a list of the top 100 downloads from the previous day, but scrolling further down the page also pulls up lists of the top 100 authors, the top 100 downloads of the last seven days and of the last 30 days.

These charts often exhibit a very populist trend, with titles such as *The Adventures of Huckleberry Finn* by Mark Twain, *The Adventures of Sherlock Holmes* by Sir Arthur Conan Doyle, *Pride and Prejudice* by Jane Austen and *A Tale of Two Cities* by Charles Dickens featuring regularly.

Project Gutenberg is not only an excellent free online resource that greatly reduces the cost of building an iPad library, but also a great way for students and anyone who would care to better themselves to catch up on the classics they may have missed.

Apple iBook store

Many of the classics available through Project Gutenberg also appear on Apple's own iBook store, which is accessed by tapping Store button at the top of the iBooks application. As with the App Store, Apple maintains download charts for both paid and free content.

Tap Top Charts on the toolbar at the bottom of the iBooks application to find them, and look in the right-hand column for the free downloads.

One of the most popular books of all time on the store is *Winnie the Pooh*, which is an excellent example of how books should be done due to its well handled graphics and text. However it's just one of thousands of ePub titles available on the store. Be aware, though, that the quality of the free books available is more varied than that of the commercial options. The less ambitious direct translations of classics such as *Pride and Prejudice* are often better about than those which draw heavily on content taken from websites and, like those titles found in Project Gutenberg, they are a great way to expand your knowledge of the great works of literature.

Kindle

Amazon clearly understood the importance of selling books through as many platforms as it could, and so as well as producing its own hardware e-book reader, called Kindle, it has created a software version of the same name which runs on the iPad, iPhone, iPod touch and other handheld devices. Like the hardware Kindle, these applications let you download free books from Amazon's online store.

To find them, launch the Kindle application and tap the 'Shop in Kindle Store' button at the top of the screen. This switches to Safari, with the Kindle Store already open. The free books are catalogued among the regular titles, but you can easily find the most popular by tapping the Top 100 Free tab on the right hand side of the screen. This initially shows you only 10 titles, but tapping the link at the bottom to see all of the bestsellers opens a new page with a more extensive list.

To download a free book, find the one you like the look of it and then tap 'Buy now with 1-Click', making sure your iPad is selected as the delivery destination below. You will not be asked to confirm, so make sure you really do want the book.

Switch back to the Kindle app and your book will download – usually, as Amazon claims, in less than 60 seconds.

Internet Archive *http://archive.org*

The Internet Archive, at archive.org is more often associated with soaring archived copies of websites for future posterity. However, the Texts section, which is accessed from the menu at the very top of the page, is also home to a wide range of more than two and a half million e-books and electronic texts. All of them are free to download.

Helpfully, these are subdivided into smaller collections, including dedicated American and Canadian libraries, Universal Library and a children's

Safety first

The Internet needn't be a scary place, but it's worth thinking twice before parting with any personal details, particularly financial ones. There are unscrupulous websites out there that promise all sorts for a software download or your credit card details. As a rule of thumb, you shouldn't need to give any personally sensitive information or download any software from the sites you visit, other than the MP3 files themselves (these will always end with .mp3).

To avoid any unwanted 'spam' email, we'd also advise you don't use your primary email address to register: either set up a free account for the purpose, such as Microsoft's Hotmail at *hotmail.co.uk*, or use a temporary account, such as one from *mailinator.com*. This will allow you to collect any registration details you need, before expiring a few hours later.

If you're entering credit card or bank details for a subscription or other purchase, you should also double-check you're using a secure site – you can tell in Safari because there will be a padlock icon at the top of the application window, while in Firefox your address bar will turn yellow. If that's not the case, the information you're entering could be intercepted.

library. You will find a considerable overlap with Project Gutenberg here, but it is still worth keeping an eye on for those titles that do not appear in the Gutenberg archive.

Open Library *http://openlibrary.org*

Open library has set itself what it calls a 'lofty but achievable goal'. It wants to create a single web page for every book ever published, and to date has gathered more than 20 million records towards the accomplishment of that goal. It works much like Wikipedia as a collaborative project to which anyone can create, add to or correct records within its database.

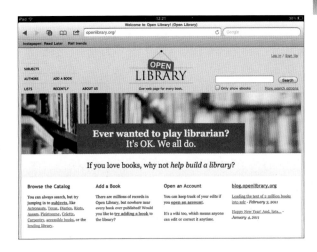

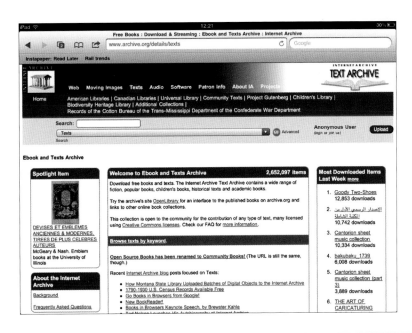

Of greatest interest, though, is its collection of e-books, which can be found by typing a title into the search box found at the top of each page and checking the box beside 'Only show ebooks'.

The results it throws up are impressive. The search for *Pride and Prejudice*, for example, brought up 753 editions of Jane Austen's work, including *Mansfield Park*, *Northanger Abbey*, *Emma*, and of course *Pride and Prejudice*. Where available as physical books there are links to buy or borrow them as appropriate, and the options for reading electronic versions are extensive. They include PDF and plain text, and two formats for iPad reading. The ePub links download versions that are compatible with the iPad's iBooks app, and a Send to Kindle option takes you back to Amazon's own website where you can choose the device that should receive the downloaded file.

Why won't my music download?

Unfortunately, there's no standard way of streaming or downloading music from a website, so you need to be selective in the formats that you download from free online libraries. One of the most common formats, MP3, is compatible with iPads, and iTunes will also convert most other formats, such as WMA files.

If you have iTunes installed, you'll have Apple's Quicktime player, too. This becomes the default player for various types of streamed media, but will usually treat any MP3 download as a stream too, preventing its download. To get around this,

load Quicktime and open its application Preferences. On the File Types tab, uncheck the boxes marked 'Streaming Audio'.

Depending on what else is installed on your PC, there may be other programs that take over when you click on a download link – RealPlayer, WinAMP and Windows Media Player, for example. If that happens, look for an option in the program to save the current media. If there isn't one, close the program, go back to the link, and right-click on it. If a Save Target As option appears, you can use this to download the MP3 file directly to your computer.

iPad reference shelf

The iPad is more than a web browser and emailing tool. Take one with you wherever you go and you'll have access to an unrivalled body of reference work thanks to these handy applications.

Remember the days when CD Rom was the future? We were amazed that you could fit a whole multi-volume encyclopedia on a single disc (these were the days before DVD).

You can still buy disc-based encyclopedias and other reference works, but why would you do that when you have an iPad at your disposal?

With a fast, wireless or 3G connection you can use your portable device to access the world's greatest online reference sources, including books, maps, atlases, dictionaries, lists of quotes and much, much more.

More interestingly, though – and more usefully – you can also download dedicated applications that either wrap up those sites in more attractive, useable interfaces, or present their own data, which isn't available elsewhere.

That's what we've done here. We have picked out eight of the best reference works for iPad owners, which when used side by side will give you a comprehensive set of reference works that can be carrier wherever you happen to travel. Try doing that with your old multi-volume set of encyclopedias and atlases... or indeed your now outdated CD Rom.

Wikipanion

Free from *bit.ly/eKaWny*

Wikipedia is widely recognised as one of the most comprehensive online reference works the world has every known. The breadth of its coverage is breathtaking, and far outranks what would ever have been possible in print to any economic degree.

It works well in the Safari browser, but the length of its pages means there are often better ways to navigate its content. Step forward Wikipanion.

This cross-device application for both the iPad and the iPhone / iPod touch is clever enough to recognise the various different parts of a Wikipedia page so that it can separate out the content from the navigation. The headings and sub-headings that appear on each page are listed in a left-hand panel, with the rest of the screen given over to displaying the content.

Tapping on the headings skips directly to the relevant part of the page you're reading, which makes it very easy to move backwards and forwards through very lengthy articles.

Linked images pop up in floating windows, which is a major improvement over the way that the website works. There, you're taken to a separate page that displays the image on its own, forcing you to step backwards through your history trail to get back to the page you were reading.

iPad 15:06 86%

Q Canterbury Cathedral

Coordinates 279722°N 1.083056°E

Contents

Canterbury Cathedral

History

Foundation by Augustine

Later Saxon and Viking periods

Norman period

Martyrdom of Thomas Becket

12th century monastery

14th-16th centuries

Dissolution of the monasteries

18th century to present

Canterbury Cathedral Appeal

The Foundation

The bells

Bibliography

Organs and organists

founded the cathedral in 602 and dedicated it to St. Saviour. Archaeological investigations under the nave floor in 1993 revealed the foundations of the original Saxon cathedral, which had been built across

County	Kent
Country	United Kingdom
Ecclesiastical information	
Denomination	Church of England
Province	Canterbury
Diocese	Canterbury

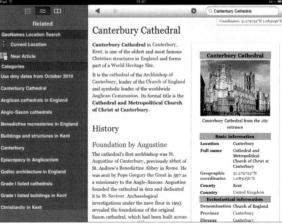

Other neat features include the ability to find articles relevant to your local area using the iPad's location-awareness features, including GPS and triangulation on the 3G mobile phone network, and the option to find articles related to the one you're reading in terms of subject and, again, location.

This free edition of Wikipanion relies on having a live Internet connection, but the £2.99 Wikipanion Plus lets you not only queue articles you want to read, but also download them, allowing you to stock up on reading material before leaving home if you only have a wifi-enabled iPad.

iPad maps and atlases

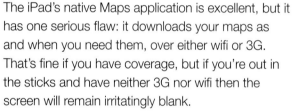

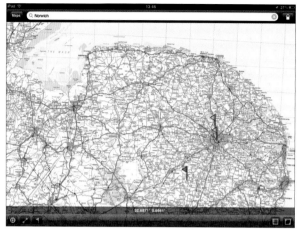

ForeverMap

59p from *bit.ly/hWbqEr*

GB Road Atlas 250K

Free from *bit.ly/elaI82*

The iPad's native Maps application is excellent, but it has one serious flaw: it downloads your maps as and when you need them, over either wifi or 3G. That's fine if you have coverage, but if you're out in the sticks and have neither 3G nor wifi then the screen will remain irritatingly blank.

ForeverMap gets around this problem by storing all of your maps locally. More than 30 countries across Europe have been mapped in their entirety, and can be downloaded one by one so that you don't fill your iPad's memory with maps of countries you'll never need.

These are more than just street plans, though, as they are enhanced by a rich selection of supplementary data. As well as Wikipedia links, there are details of shops, services, restaurants, cafes and attractions in each city, each of which can be used as a reference point for mapping.

ForeverMap uses maps from the OpenStreetMap project which, like Wikipedia, is an enormous collaborative project that over recent years has reached a level where it can rival commercial alternatives. The only complaint we can level at it is the fact that the maps don't look as good as the native application's equivalents, but when you're lost in the woods and this is your only hope of getting home safely, will you really care? All that matters is their clarity, which is excellent.

There's something comforting about an Ordnance Survey map. Their careful lines, measured colours and immediate familiarity to anyone who has grown up in the United Kingdom make their inclusion in any application running on the iPad very tempting.

This app is a version of RouteBuddy Solo, and includes the 1:250,000 scale map of the whole of the country. That's not the most detailed version available, but it's good enough to accurately plot your current location and put it in context.

It uses your iPad's navigation tools, including the GPS receiver, to track your movements, showing not only where you are, but even where you're facing. Tap a button and it'll save your movements as a route, which can be recalled later.

There's a very simple but smart padlock tool that freezes the map on the screen in its current position and locks your iPad, with a slider like the one used to turn it on displayed at the bottom of the screen. This lets you put your iPad aside while you do other things, safe in the knowledge that you'll still know where you are when you come back to it.

This is just one element in a suite of Ordnance Survey maps from app creator RouteBuddy. If the scale is simply not fine enough for your needs then a link from within the application itself takes you to the RouteBuddy site, and from there to the App Store to buy more detailed alternatives.

Google Earth
Free from *bit.ly/gqyE4n*

Google Earth has quickly established itself as the best free application-based mapping tool on the Mac and PC, and now it's come to the iPad.

Like the regular edition it starts with a view of the spinning globe, which can be dragged by swiping with a single finger and zoomed by pinching and unpinching.

The level of detail available varies depending on the part of the world you have chosen to view, but on those parts that have been photographed in high resolution, you can easily pick out individual vehicles driving along roads.

It can pinpoint your location to within a few metres and plot locally-relevant Wikipedia entries,

which can make for a fascinating few hours of tapping through your neighbourhood, learning about your surroundings.

This is more than a flat mapping tool, though. It is entirely photo-based, and optionally uses the iPad's accelerometer to register the orientation of your device to render the terrain at a tilt that matches the angle to which you're holding it. Keep it level and you'll enjoy a bird's-eye view; tilt it upright and you'll look across the landscape towards the horizon.

The speed and responsiveness of this application on a decent home broadband connection is impressive, and makes it as much an entertainment app as it is a reference work.

Weather Pro for iPad

£2.99 from *bit.ly/fUT1ie*

So much of our lives relies on the weather. Sports events, long walks, gardening, boat trips, long drives, holidays... the weather touches just about everything we do, every day.

That's why knowing what we're facing is often so important, and why we have invested so much as a species in the technology we need to make reliable forecasts. WeatherPro makes use of those forecasts to draw up extensive and genuinely useful graphical projections of the week ahead.

It can work out your current location and build a forecast on this basis, or you can search for specific cities, which will be added to a scrollable list of saved locations.

With your chosen location selected, WeatherPro displays not only upcoming temperature and rainfall, but wind speed and direction, humidity, UV levels and air pressure. In every case, each statistic is presented in numeric form below a simple graph that gives you an at-a-glance of the situation. By reading these graphs across the full width of the screen you get a clear image of how the weather is going to change over the course of the week.

Crucially, it doesn't just present averages. The temperature graph shows maximum, minimum and 'feels like' figures, while the wind speed graph shows both the average speed and maximum gust speeds, which are frequently much higher and can be more damaging than a steady ongong breeze.

If your life relies in any way on knowing what the weather holds in store, WeatherPro is for you.

Chambers Dictionary

£4.99 from *bit.ly/e7VMTA*

The English language is among the most extensive and flexible used anywhere in the world.

With such a large vocabulary and many irregular verbs it can be difficult to learn, and even those of us who count it as our mother tongue often find ourselves using two words where one would do – or using the wrong word altogether.

A good dictionary will go a long way to improving and correcting your use of the language, and there are few dictionaries better than Chambers. The distinctive red-backed volumes are clear, comprehensive and contemporary, and favoured by many writers,

The iPad version may not have a red cover, but it does nod at the volume's heritage, with a red splash screen in the this edition, and a picture of the book itself on the iPhone. Once open, the quality of its content shines through. Chambers' developers haven't tried to impress us with a fancy interface, instead letting the words themselves take centre stage. A simple search box lets you look up words, with possible matches displayed in a list and the definitions themselves given the lion's share of the window. As well as meanings, this shows alternative uses, related words and etymological roots, to provide a thorough understanding of each one.

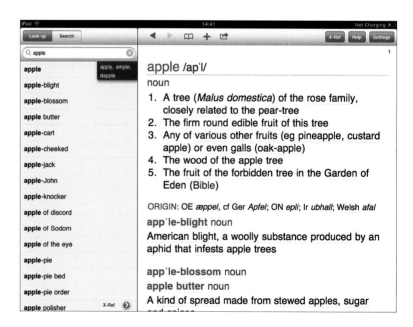

Chambers Thesaurus

£2.99 from *bit.ly/g7hJPu*

Chambers Thesaurus is the perfect companion to its dictionary product. Not only is it an equally extensive reference work and a blessing for writers and poets looking for alternatives to their tired, over-used words, but it's also directly linked to the dictionary.

Tapping the X-Ref button in the Chambers Dictionary application calls up a list of online and offline sources that you can use to further your understanding of the word in question. One of the offline sources is Chambers Thesaurus which, when tapped, opens the same word in this app. You can perform the same action in reverse direction, too, tapping X-Ref in the thesaurus to check the currently displayed word in the dictionary.

Aside from the cross referencing, the search tools make this app far more useful than a printed alternative, allowing you to search for partial words with missing letters, specifying that those letters should be consonants, vowels, any single letter or a multiple but unknown number of letters. For crossword players this will help no end with tricky clues, even if it does smack slightly of cheating.

If you've never had much use for a thesaurus, this app will likely convert you. At £2.99 it also represents excellent value for money.

GoSkyWatch Planetarium

Free from *bit.ly/fWLU2x*

Most of us can recognise at least a few constellations, simply from having seen them every day of our lives for so many years.

The heavens above us are are infinite and growing, though, so none of us could ever hope to name every star that passes above our heads.

With GoSkyWatch you don't need to. Simply hold your iPad above your head so that its back points to the star you want to name. You'll see a full recreation of the sky above you shown on the iPad screen, with a target at the centre. As this crosses on each star or planet their names pop up beside them. So, too, do the constellations, which are drawn as proper pictures, rather than a loose collection of spots in the sky.

The clever thing is that by knowing where you are and the time of the day it can plot not only the visible sky, but also the astrological view on the other side of the planet if you hold it down towards your feet. Likewise, it will show you which stars feature in our own sky in the middle of the day. They're invisible to us because of the brightness of the sun, but they're there nonetheless.

As well as naming the stars and planets you can see yourself, it will tell you where to look to spot a specific celestial body. Categorised into planets, constellations, deep sky objects and individual stars, tapping one calls up visual directions, showing you which way to look to find it in either hemisphere. Even if you have no interest in astronomy, this is a truly fascinating application.

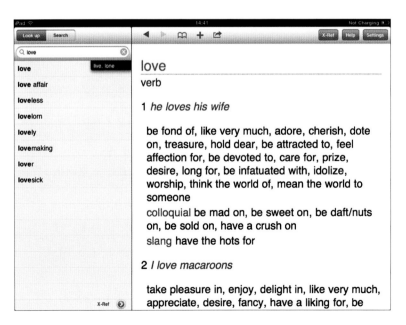

Chapter 4
Everything iPad

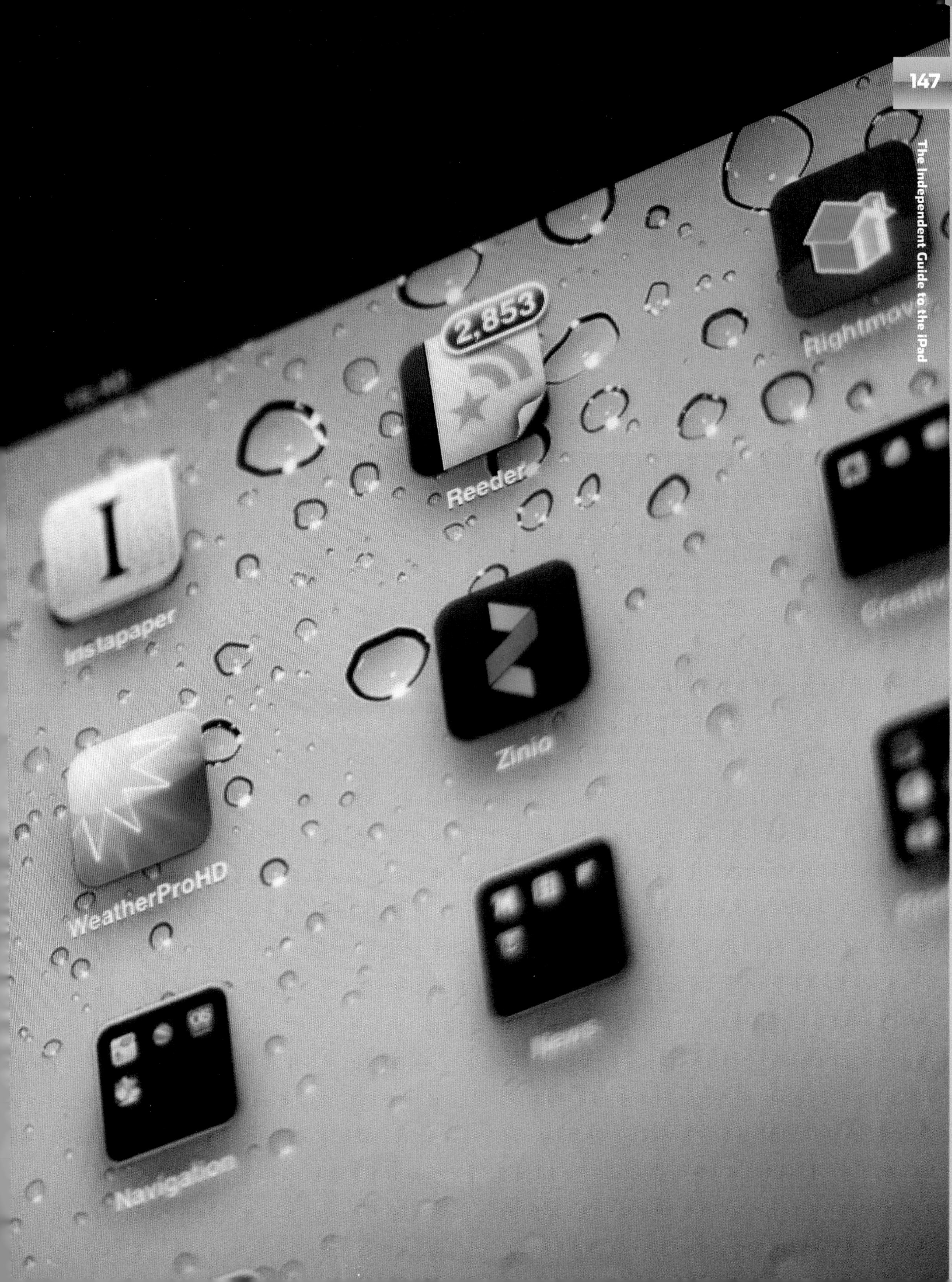
2,853
Reeder
Instapaper
Zinio
WeatherProHD
Navigation

iPad accessories

The iPad is the centre of a whole world of accessories and add-ons. Here we highlight some of the best and most desirable optional extras that will enhance your tablet experience.

Joby Ori for iPad

joby.com/gorillamobile/ori
£79.95

Is it a case, or is it a stand? Take your pick. The Ori is one of the most versatile iPad accessories money can buy – it's both.

Joby is best-known for its smart pliable camera stands that work just as well hanging from a branch as they do standing on a table, so it's no surprise to see the same lateral thinking applied to the iPad.

Ori was 'inspired by origami', hence the name, and while it folds shut to become a sleek folio case, it can also open up to support your iPad at an angle for comfortable typing or stand upright to raise your tablet up to eye level.

It's built from a strong yet lightweight aluminium composite, so it not only looks good, but is tough, too. It will protect your iPad with aplomb, and won't weigh down your bag in the process.

Closed, it's just 7.8 x 0.9 x 10.9in in size, which is impressively compact when you consider that it can hoist your iPad to a height of 14in.

Combine a stand like this with a Bluetooth keybord, such as the BTKeyMini from Macally, profiled over the page, and you will transform your iPad from a handy on-the-go web and apps tool into a fully-fledged mobile office that saves on space and will synchronise with your Mac or PC when you get back to your desk.

FreeLoader Classic

solartechnology.com
£39.99

The iPad's 10 hour battery life is a corker, but there's still a chance you'll find yourself away from base at precisely the moment it needs plugging in. Well fear not: help is at hand with this smart portable solar cell charging set.

FreeLoader Classic now sports more efficient cells, which collect 25% more power from the available light, so should be more effective in cloudier climes. These charge an internal battery, which can then be plugged in to any USB-charged device, including the iPhone, Sony PSP, Nintendo DS and, crucially, the iPad. As these devices slowly drain the battery they'll keep running and you will stay productive.

The smart design lays flat when the cells are extended – like the foils on a satellite – so could be laid out on a windowsill, or the parcel shelf or dashboard of a parked car. There's a handy LCD display on the central housing that shows you the level of charge in the battery, the current power input and your active connections. The really impressive thing, though, is its stamina.

Its manufacturer claims that a fully charged FreeLoader Classic will power an iPod or iPhone for 18 hours, a regular smartphone for 44 hours, a PSP or DS for two and a half hours and an iPad for two hours. This should be enough to see you through the last leg of a tedious flight, or keep you working through a busy meeting when you're away from your desk and its accompanying power points.

It comes with a selection of adaptors for use with a range of devices, and there are accessories, too. The Supercharger, for example, shortens the length of time it takes the FreeLoader to charge, which will be a boon for travellers. It is also tough and weather-resistant, so can be attached to the outside of a rucksack to passively charge the battery while you're out and about on a hike. It is available separately or as a pack with the Classic.

There are other reasons to look towards the FreeLoader Classic, though: green reasons. Investing in a battery pack of this sort means that we can harness a financially free and pollution free source of energy, so the long-term savings won't only be economical, but also ecological.

Macally Viewstand

macally-europe.com

€59.95

You may wonder how something so simple can be so versatile, but when you've spent a few minutes playing with the Viewstand you'll wonder no more.

To start with, it looks great. The muted aluminium construction is the perfect compliment to the iPad itself. With smoothly-rounded corners and a precision-rolled elbow it's also highly reminiscent of an iMac or Cinema Display, so will look great on any desk beside a regular Apple computer.

But the Viewstand is about more than just good looks. That simple curve in its simple construction is designed to support your iPad in four different orientations. As well as the vertical, portrait orientation shown here it will support it in a vertical landscape orientation, and both landscape and portrait at a shallow angle, tilted up from your desk to facilitate efficient, comfortable typing. Particularly heavy iPad users can keep their device plugged in while using the stand.

At a suggested retail price of €60 it isn't cheap, but it's clearly built to last, and you'll enjoy years of daily use from this handy, stylish, sleek device.

Macally Airpouch

macally-europe.com

€29.95

This smart, slimline pouch is a supremely stylish way to protect your iPad from the bumps and scratches it might otherwise sustain from days spent tucked away in your work bag.

Soft and light, it's made from durable nylon and has a soft-touch lining to keep your iPad's glass screen and aluminium back protected. With a total of three storage pouches it could be just what you need to organise every part of your mobile life.

Macally BTKeyMini

macally-europe.com
€79.95

The iPad's on-screen keyboard is great, but if you're set on typing several thousand words it pays to splash out on a proper external device. This Bluetooth add-on works at a distance of up to 10m, has volume controls, 77 keys and a set of AAA batteries thrown in to get you going.

It works with any device running iOS 4.0 or above, including the iPhone and iPod touch, and with a Bluetooth-equipped computer running Mac OS X 10.2.8 or later, so once you get used to its dimensions and layout you can use it on a Mac, too.

You won't realise how much of a difference it makes switching to a regular keyboard, but it really does make your iPad a proper mobile computer.

Macally Shellstand

macally-europe.com
€49.95

Can't decide between a case and a stand? Now you don't need to. The Macally Shellstand rotates your iPad through 180 degrees and supports both landscape and portrait orientation so you can use your tablet in whichever mode best suits the active application.

A ridged strip running down the centre of the base lets you change the angle at which the iPad is held and, perhaps most importantly, the stand itself can be removed, leaving you with a supremely portable case for your device.

Made from rigid silicon, the Shellstand is as protective as it is versatile, and will keep your iPad safe when you're on out and about, making this the perfect add-on for any mobile worker.

Griffin PowerDock Dual

griffintechnology.com
$34.99

Apple devices are addictive. As soon as you have one you'll want to buy another. And another, and another... the list goes on until you have so much Apple kit on your desk you'll be struggling for space... and for sockets with which to charge them.

The PowerDock Dual goes some way to solving this problem, allowing you to dock an iPhone and iPad at the same time, charging them from a singe connection through the power input at the back of the elegantly curved base.

A highly versatile solution, as well as the iPad and iPhone the PowerDock Dual will take everything from the iPod touch to the three most recent nano models in its stride. It will even work with the chunky, capacious iPod classic for those who can't bear to leave even the smallest portion of their music collection at home.

For anyone with more than one iDevice and a paucity of plugs it's a must-have add-on.

Sennheiser MM 70i

sennheiser.co.uk
£69.99

Not just a set of ear buds, this impressive kit sports three buttons on the casing that let you control your iPad, iPhone or iPod without looking at the screen.

With effective noise blocking you'll be able to listen to your music properly without turning up the volume to ear-splitting levels, as it won't be interrupted by the sound of the car, train or plane in which you're riding. This, in turn, should help to preserve the life of your precious battery.

Sennheiser claims that sound is more natural and lifelike, thanks in part to the fact that they come with three sizes of ear buds in two different shapes to help you find the perfect fit for your particular ears

With a two year international warranty, they provide quality listening alongside peace of mind.

Cygnett iPad 2 cases

cygnett.com
£34.95

These beautiful cases for the sleek iPad 2 come in a range of colours and are improved editions of the company's most popular cases for the bulkier original iPad.

Our favourite is certainly this smart glossy red, but they also come in leather and armoured finishes to protect your tablet from bumps, dents and scratches.

With a smart and simple angled cover they can be used in either orientation as an opening book or propped-up stand for working on the move – particularly if you also have a keyboard, in which case they form the bedrock of your mobile office.

The cases leave all ports unobstructed so you won't need to remove your iPad to plug it in or use the headphone port, and because they have a hidden magnet in the surround they'll stay neatly shut without any visible buckles or straps.

Scosche goBAT II

scosche.com
£69.99

The iPad has a great battery. It'll sleep for weeks and run for days between charges. How often, though, do you find yourself at some inconvenient location when it starts to run dry?

Save yourself the frustration of a boring commuter or flight without a working iPad by investing in the Scosche goBAT II. This handy, sleek device contains a 5000mAh rechargable battery that you'll power up before leaving your home or office. Once you hit the road you can use your iPad however you like, with the assurance that should you run the internal battery dry the goBAT II will come to your aid.

It has two USB ports in one end, with one rated at 10 Watts (2.1 Amp) to charge your iPad, and the other at 5 Watts (1 Amp) for other common gadgets such as an iPhone or iPod. There's even an adaptor

for the increasingly popular Samsung Galaxy Tab, should you be travelling with anyone who has bought themselves an alternative tablet device.

The goBAT II ships with a micro USB cable for charging the battery itself, which can also be used for subsequently charging any device that uses this kind of connection as its power source. It works with reVIVE, a free charging app that tells you how long a device will take to charge using a Scosche charger and will, optionally, send you an email when the charging cycle has completed, to save you the chore of waiting for it to finish.

If you're a serious iPad user then a spare battery is a boon. This one's good looks are a bonus.

How did we get here?

The iPad was a long time coming. It's the result of several years' development of many different products, but how did the tablet computer we now know so well come into being?.

Apple's first foray into the world of tablet computing came in the form of its Newton platform. Primitive by todays's standards, but an impressive achievement in the 1990s, the Newton OS and the MessagePad devices that it powered shared much in common with iOS and the iPad.

Over 11 years, from 1987 until 1998, Apple produced six handheld MessagePad devices and one eMate, which was more akin to a modern-day netbook computer. The eMate was the only device to feature a keyboard, but the MessagePad devices worked with handwriting recognition, allowing users to scribble directly onto the screen and have their jottings translated into recognisable, neatly-typed text – without a keyboard.

The devices had a range of built-in applications, which could be supplemented by further apps installed by the end user, as is the case with the iPad. In one key respect, though, they differed significantly: the MessagePad relied on a stylus for user input whereas the iPad is entirely finger-driven.

The Newton line-up flourished during the reign of Gil Amelio, but when Steve Jobs returned to the company as CEO he cancelled the project. That wasn't the end of the story, though.

Two Newton developers went on to found a company called Pixo. It developed operating systems for small devices, including mobile phones, and was eventually bought by Sun Microsystems. Before that happened, though, it had been approached by Apple to work on another project: the operating system for the original iPod. That

operating system is still used in some of the current iPod models being shipped. The iPod, then, has an even stronger connection to the iPad than we may already have suspected.

It may be the iMac that made Apple interesting again and set us all looking at its computer line-up once more, but it was the iPod that revived its fortunes. Looking back at the first iPod, it's easy to see why it wasn't an immediate success. It had a FireWire interface, a capacity of just 5GB – enough to store 1000 songs – and was Mac compatible. *Only* Mac compatible. It took a while for Apple to cotton on to the fact that the iPod alone wouldn't be enough to drive significant Mac sales in those early days (unlike now) and that if it wanted to make a success of its first true 'post-PC platform' it would have to open it up to just that – the PC.

That happened in July 2002 when Apple unveiled its second-generation player. It would play happily with Windows 2000 or later, but was still primitive compared to the touch-and-swipe devices we've come to know and love today.

The mechanical scroll wheel of the first edition had been swapped out for a touch-sensitive equivalent with four buttons around the edge for playing, pausing and skipping tracks forwards and backwards, pointing towards today's fully-swipable surfaces. The capacity had been boosted to a maximum of 20GB – enough for 4000 songs.

It took until September 2007 for Apple to come up with the iPod touch, which is the closest it had got by that point to replicating some of the features

It may not look much like an iPad, but the original iPod, which had a capacity of just 5GB – or 1000 songs – and lacked a touch-sensitive screen was the first step on a long road of development that ends up where we are today: with the stunning full-colour 9.7in iPad 2. Over the years we have seen its buttons rationalised, the screen switch from monochrome to colour, and the operating system advance to the point where we can now install our own choice of applications, downloaded directly from Apple's walled, fully-checked App Store. It has also, crucially, switched from being a Mac-only device to a gadget that's equally happy talking to Windows running on a PC.

of a traditional Personal Digital Assistant (PDA) on an iPod, with a large screen that could be used simultaneously to display content and accept input.

By then, though, the first-generation iPhone was already shipping, and although the iPod touch was an impressive piece of kit it was out on a spur as far as the iPad's evolution is concerned.

The iPhone had been much discussed before Apple ever admitted that it was anything other than a nice idea. Countless mock-ups had appeared over the years as magazines, analysts and fans speculated over its final appearance. Nobody had dared suggest that it would be as advanced as it turned out to be.

The rest of the mobile phone world found itself backfooted. Other manufacturers were still relying on a face full of buttons and keys to operate their hardware and integrated software.

The iPhone, though, did away with all but the home button, mute switch and volume rocker. It was such a successful implementation that those very same buttons remain the only physical controls on the iPad 2 (although the function of the 'mute' switch is a user-controlled selection – you can opt for mute, or a way of locking the screen so that it doesn't rotate when you turn the device on its side).

The iPhone was such a phenomenal success that every device from any rival that bore more than a passing resemblance was mooted as a possible 'iPhone killer'. As we now know, few of them ever came close to achieving that aim, and the iPhone remains one of the best-selling handsets ever.

Having got this far, producing the iPad was largely a matter of scale. It may lack the iPhone's voice transport features and text messaging, but in many other respects the iPad and iPhone share many common features. They both use the same operating system – iOS 4.3 at the time the iPad 2 shipped – and can run many of the same applications. 65,000 entries on the App Store have been adapted to take advantage of the iPad's larger screen without scaling up the limited number of pixels found on the original iPhone and iPod touch, meaning it's now possible to use the devices side by side, with each running software that's compatible with both platforms.

Apple has come full circle. It may have canned its first tablet PC project, but the move has been proved inspired. By stepping away from the Newton line, it freed itself to work on a whole range of more profitable products that have produced an ecosystem that runs from the iPod shuffle nano and touch, though the iPhone and on to the iPad. The only question is where the company goes from here.

What happens next?

iPad 2 was a very logical next step from the original iPad, but it's certainly not the point at which Apple will stop developing its revolutionary tablet device. What might iPad 3 and beyond hold in store for us?

Apple defined its own benchmark with the original iPad. We had all seen iPhones and the iPod touch before, but none of us really knew how well the technology would scale up to the point where it occupied such a large screen. The results were better than we could have imagined. Its success was all but guaranteed. So was the fact that Apple would follow up with a second generation – and probably other models further down the line.

Some logical changes that might have come along with iPad 2 never appeared, though. While the front- and rear-mounted cameras were pretty much a given considering how hard Apple is pushing FaceTime on the iPhone 4, iPod touch and Mac, and an improved processor was a logical next step, those who had been looking to the iPhone for further clues about what might happen next would probably have found themselves wrong-footed.

In the step from iPhone to iPhone 3 (there was no iPhone 2), Apple moved away from the metal back casing, instead choosing to house the smartphone's smartest components behind a gently curved plastic cover. Would it do the same with the iPad? Apparently not, and with good reason. Apple has developed a technology that it calls Unibody, which lets it sculpt the casings of its notebook computers from a single piece of drilled metal. It has applied this to iPad 2 with stunning results, allowing it to slim it right down. If it had switched to plastic it would probably have had to use a thicker material, thus negating the point of the whole slimming exercise. It wouldn't have looked nearly so

'premium', either, dramatically cheapening the look of the finished product. For this reason, we probably shouldn't expect such a back to form part of the iPad 3, either. Many of Apple's competitors have opted for fully plastic cases in an effort to drive down prices, and Apple will likely want to differentiate itself from them.

Further, Apple has managed to maintain its high build quality without increasing the price of the second-generation iPad beyond that which it charged for the original unit. This is a serious point in Apple's favour, and something of which CEO Steve Jobs made a point when he unveiled the iPad 2. As he explained at the launch event, most of Apple's competitors are struggling to produce even one tablet that they can sell at less than $799, while Apple itself has five iPads below this price point and only one above it.

We should therefore not expect iPad 3 to be significantly more expensive than iPad 2.

Neither should we expect a proliferation of wild colours. Apple's industrial design is classy and conservative. Its computers now come in just two colours – white or aluminium – and while the lower-end 'consumer' iPods such as the shuffle and nano sport a wide range of colours, the more serious entertainment and communication devices in its line-up – the iPhone and iPod touch – come in just black, or black and white. As a premium product, the iPad is aligned more closely to the iPhone than the low-end iPod, and so we should expect it to maintain its current cool appearance, with cases such as the SmartCover used as the primary means of adding a touch of colour to the line-up.

So far we have talked a lot about what *won't* happen when the iPad 3 arrives, but what *will* happen, and should you hold off on buying a new iPad until it appears?

Taking a level, analytical view of the line-up as it stands, if you already have an original iPad then it's probably worth skipping a generation and waiting for iPad 3 before you upgrade. Apple has shipped a free operating system update for iPad 1 users, and although the device lacks iPad 2's cameras, thus putting both FaceTime and PhotoBooth out of reach, only the most demanding of users would be able to justify the cost of a brand new tablet purely for the speed benefits delivered by the faster processor and improved graphics performance. If you don't already have an iPad, though, now is a great time to buy your first model.

So, what improvements might we expect to see in iPad 3? Seasoned industry watchers will know how difficult it is to second-guess Apple's next move on any front, but we can make some deductions on the basis of what was missing from iPad 2.

Chief among these was the retina display of the iPhone 4 – and even, now, the iPod touch. When you first see this close-up you'll understand what a difference it makes to cram 326 pixels into each linear inch. You really can't make out each one individually, and the result is an incredibly crisp display.

If Apple was to apply the same pixel density to the iPad 3 it would sport a resolution of roughly 1890 x 2542 pixels, which easily rivals many desktop monitors. With some clever scaling iOS would be able to render interface elements more smoothly than before while still displaying fonts at easily legible sizes.

Further use of gestures will almost certainly be on the cards. At the moment the iPad actually lags behind Apple's conventional computers where its MacBooks' built-in trackpads, and the external Magic Trackpad and Magic Mouse give users the ability to swipe around the operating system, activating interface tools like Expose to display running applications and navigating through browser history lists. Porting an Expose equivalent to iOS would allow for more elegant application switching in the multitasking environment than the current double-clicking of the home button, which in turn may inspire it to lose that button altogether. Would it then go on to get rid of the bezel? Probably not, as we'd have no part of the device where we could hold it without obscuring part of the display.

It will continue to update iOS. At the time of writing it stands at version 4.3, but as the hardware in the iPad, iPhone and iPod continues to evolve, so will the software that controls it. This will mean, inevitably, that older iPads, including the original, will likely become obsoleted as the years go by. This, more than any hardware development, will likely be the biggest inducement to upgrade that any of us is likely to see.

Taking things further

Still have a question you need answering? Looking for up-to-date news and reviews? Want to connect with like-minded users? Check out these websites for more daily stimulation for any iPad owner.

MacUser

From the same publishing house as this book, MacUser's website is updated daily with the latest news and views on all things Mac, including the iPhone, iPod and iPad.

MacUser is the UK's longest-running Mac magazine and the only one to publish every fortnight, meaning it can bring you the latest reviews and breaking news first. Join its team of expert writers online and keep up to date with everything that's happening in the world of Apple and iPad.

macuser.co.uk

Apple's official iPad pages

Apple's own site is an obvious place to start. It's the only official source of information for iPad news, so if there's anything to talk about, this is where you'll hear it – or read it – first. The pages are fairly nationalised to cater for each market, so it's worth visiting your local version. In the US, this is *apple.com/ipad*, whereas in the UK it is *apple.com/uk/ipad*.

Keep in mind, of course, that the iPad pages are focused on one objective entirely, and that is selling iPads. They aren't how-to pages or troubleshooting guides. They can be found elsewhere in Apple's support documentation.

apple.com/ipad

PC Pro

Windows users should check out MacUser's sister title, PC Pro. With one of the best-resourced editorial teams in technology journalism, it is the authoritative voice on all things IT.

pcpro.co.uk

The Unofficial Apple Weblog

Part of AOL, The Unofficial Apple Weblog reports anything and everything to do with Apple, and maintains its own dedicated iPad pages in a separate category. It's a mixture of news and tips, threading together new application release announcements, handy hints and breaking stories. It also has a useful tip of the day box and featured galleries, so there's plenty to see.

tuaw.com/category/ipad

Glossary

The iPad is a supremely friendly piece of kit, but the world it inhabits is populated by unfamiliar words and acronyms. Here are some of the most common terms you'll come across in daily iPad use.

AAC

Advanced Audio Codec (AAC) is the preferred format for music storage in iTunes and on the iPod. It is also the standard format for music tracks (although not Podcasts) downloaded from the iTunes Music Store. It can be converted to MP3 for greater cross-platform compatibility.

AIFF

Audio Interchange File Format, developed by Apple in 1988 and most commonly used on its range of Mac computers.

Album Art

Iconised versions of album and single covers downloaded automatically at the same time as music bought from the iTunes Music Store. This is displayed in a pane on the iTunes interface, on the screens of iPods (except iPod shuffle) and, of course, the iPad, during track playback. Album art can also be added to tracks you have ripped yourself, either by scanning the artwork or by tasking an application such as CoverScout to source them for you from the web.

Audiobooks

Specially formatted audio files (not necessarily books) that allow for bookmarking. Stopping playback of an audiobook track at any point will save your position so that when you resume playing the next time you'll pick up at the same place.

Bit rate

Means of expressing the number of audio samples processed in a set period of time, usually a second. See also KBPS.

Capacity

The amount of data that can be held by your iPad. This will be slightly smaller than the stated capacity of the iPad itself due to the way capacities are measured and space consumed by iOS.

Dock

Small brick-like device with a slot for the iPad to sit in. Inside the slot is a connector that exactly matches that on the end of an iPad data cable. Sitting the iPad in the Dock both charges it and updates its contents. Apple produces two Docks for the iPad, with one sporting an integrated keyboard, which turns the iPad into a compact desktop computer for daily use.

DRM

Digital Rights Management. A range of systems that control how digital content can be used and how many times it can be copied. It protects music creators' and publishers' copyrights. Now largely less restrictive than it once was.

FairPlay

The DRM system used by iTunes and the associated Music Store. It is used to protect some

AAC-encoded audio files and was, some say, key to the success of the iPod, as only iTunes-compatible players such as the iPod could play back FairPlay-protected music tracks.

GB

Gigabyte. Roughly one billion bytes, where one byte is equivalent to a single character, such as the letter 'a' stored on a disk. It is a measurement of data capacity, and is the terminology used when describing the capacity of the iPad.

H.264

High quality digital video format that allows videos to be highly compressed while retaining as high a quality as possible. Widely used by Apple and YouTube, and likely to become more popular with mass adoption of HTML5.

iPhone

All-in-one communications and entertainment device from Apple, produced as a follow-up to its phenomenally successful iPod line of portable music players. It was developed amid utmost secrecy, and finally revealed to the public in January 2007, following massive blog and media speculation. As well as regular telephony features, it incorporates an address book, music and video player, mapping application and full-blown email client, with push-email services similar to those found on a Blackberry communications device.

iPod

As well as a generic term used to describe Apple's range of portable music players and the equivalent playback software on the iPhone and iPad it is, more specifically, how Apple describes the full-sized, top-end player in its range, now called the classic.

iTunes

Apple software for both PCs and Macs used to download, store and play back music, interact with its own online music store and transfer tracks and data to and from an iPad. On the iPad it is used entirely for the downloads and management, not for media playback.

Kbps

Kilobits per second. A measurement of the number of audio samples that go to make up each second of music in a digitally-encoded track. The higher this number, the smoother the file will be reproduced.

Lossless

Level of compression that has no discernable impact on the quality of the audio file, despite some data being discarded during the encoding process.

MB

Megabyte: one million bytes, where one byte is a single character, such as the letter 'a'. Used to measure the capacity of a device, such as the iPad, an iPod or a USB memory key.

MobileMe

Online service run by Apple to provide a range of features of use to Mac and PC owners, including email, online storage, calendar synchronisation across multiple machines and basic backup tools. On a Mac it appears as a connected drive, and on all platforms it can be used as an online storage area for personal files and folders. Its email service is Imap-based, meaning that users' mail accounts will always be in the same state, reflecting the same read and unread messages, on any device used to access the service. It replaced the ageing .Mac service that was compatible with the first iPhone.

MP3

Dominant form of audio compression, and the name that people give to files compressed in this way. Unpopular among many recording industry executives as it is difficult to impose copyright restriction measures on this format. This is the mostcommon format for podcasts, and can be played by the iPad and iPod.

Multitouch

Name given to Apple's technology for implementing on-screen actions by moving fingers around a seemingly inflexible display, such as that found on the iPad, iPhone and iPod touch.

Playlist

List of tracks drawn from one or more albums that will be played either in sequence or a random order, or burned to disc through the iTunes interface or iPod application. Playlists can be copied between iTunes and the iPad, allowing you to take 'virtual' albums on the move.

Podcast

Non-live radio style broadcast downloaded through the iTunes podcast directory in the Music Store. Quality is highly variable. However, the likes of the BBC and Penguin Books have long seen the benefit of podcasting, which means a wide range of high quality material is now available.

Pop3

Predominant technology for email delivery used by most consumer ISPs. iPad compatible.

Push email

Technology by which emails are sent from the central server that holds them to a client device, such as a mobile phone or iPad, without the owner having to manually instigate a retrieval.

QuickTime

Video format developed by Apple. Closely tied in to iTunes software, and shipped with all Macintosh computers. It is required by iTunes to play back videos, and is a popular format for professional video production.

Rip

To extract audio from a CD for digital playback from a computer, or a portable device such as the iPhone or iPad.

Sync

Contraction of synchronise. To copy data from iTunes to an iPad, and pass other data back to the computer, such as the number of times a track has been played from the iPad.

USB 2.0

Hi speed connection method used to link iPads and either PCs or Macs. This replaced the FireWire cables used to connect older iPods and many video cameras, serving to make them more universally compatible.

Wifi

Once colloquial, but now generally-accepted term for wireless networking. It embodies several standards, of which the four most common are 802.11a, 802.11b, 802.11g and 802.11n. The 802.11a and 802.11g standards can each achieve a peak throughput of 54megabits/second. 802.11b runs at 11megabits/second. 802.11n, the fastest standard at 248megabits/second, is unratified, although draft standards have allowed it to be built into many wireless devices already, giving it good overall industry support. The iPad supports 802.11b, g and n.

Wireless Access Point

Device that connects your network or broadband connection to your iPad and other computers.